Anita Hemphill is an instructor at the University of California, Los Angeles (UCLA). **Charles Hemphill, Jr.** is the author of PRACTICAL GUIDE TO REAL ESTATE LAW (Prentice-Hall, Inc.).

Kathy Ellenbaas
to Choices 1992

Information Provided by:
CHOICES of [illegible] County, Inc.
Office [illegible]-6997
Crisis 1-800-723-[illegible] or 201-723-6004

Prentice-Hall, Inc. Englewood Cliffs, N.J. 07632

Anita M. Hemphill
Charles F. Hemphill, Jr.

Womanlaw

a guide to legal matters vital to women

Library of Congress Cataloging in Publication Data

Hemphill, Charles F.
Womanlaw, a guide for legal matters vital to women.

(A Spectrum Book)
Includes index.
1. Women—Legal status, laws, etc.—United States.
I. Hemphill, Anita M. II. Title.
KF478.H45 346.7301'34 81-8619

ISBN 0-13-961847-3 {PBK}

ISBN 0-13-961854-6

A SPECTRUM BOOK

10 9 8 7 6 5 4 3 2 1

Printed in the United States of America

Editorial production/supervision
and interior design by Cyndy Lyle Rymer

Manufacturing buyer: Barbara Frick

Prentice-Hall International, Inc., *London*
Prentice-Hall of Australia Pty. Limited, *Sydney*
Prentice-Hall of Canada, Ltd., *Toronto*
Prentice-Hall of India Private Limited, *New Delhi*
Prentice-Hall of Japan, Inc., *Tokyo*
Prentice-Hall of Southeast Asia Pte. Ltd., *Singapore*
Whitehall Books Limited, *Wellington, New Zealand*

Contents

Preface

This book is addressed to all women—single, married, divorced, widowed, rich, poor, young, elderly, middle-aged. Today, more and more women are taking responsibility for their own lives and for understanding their own situations. And increasing numbers of women are encountering legal entanglements.

At the same time, remarkable changes are taking place in society. More women have responsibility as the head of a household. A considerable number are taking an important role in their families' financial support. And increasing segments of society are acknowledging the legal inequalities that exist.

Some aspects of the law primarily concern women: social security and pension rights for widows, laws dealing with violence against women, the question of pregnancy leave, and others. But some common legal problems interest the many women who wish to better understand their own rights and obligations. And in some instances, the laws governing these common situations treat men and women differently.

This book has been designed as a handbook and guide to legal questions and problems that are most likely to have an effect on a woman's life. It outlines basic principles of law and clears away pitfalls, especially those most likely to cause problems. Naturally, a book of this kind cannot be all-inclusive. The laws that relate to women's rights are now so numerous that a small library would barely hold all the volumes. In many instances, specific facts make a woman's problem somewhat unique. And because changes in economic, social, and political views influence judges and lawmakers, laws vary from state to state and from time to time. Frequently, only an attorney can advise you what to do in a specific situation.

You can handle some legal matters yourself, but others are best left to an attorney. This book was written to furnish a bridge of information between you and that attorney.

Although no book can ever substitute for a lawyer, this material can clarify many basic legal situations and help you to determine if you ought to consult an attorney. Law often seems an overly complicated field. But by remaining informed and by understanding basic legal principles, you can be a far more knowledgeable client for the attorney who helps you to protect your legal rights.

Every effort has been made to use nonlegal, clear language when possible and to include the most recent laws and legislative proposals affecting women.

We wish to thank Cary Franklin, A.S.A., for help and constructive advice. We are also grateful to Carol Chase of the California Bar and to Ross H. Hemphill of the Texas Bar. Margaret A. Morse was of considerable assistance in manuscript preparation.

chapter 1

Introduction

So long as one segment of society has limited rights, none of us is completely free. In most eras and in most cultures, woman has been seen (and in many ways still is seen) as subordinate to man. Identical rights simply never existed in the past. And in spite of the rhetoric and the changes in recent years, legal equality has not yet become part of everyday reality.

This book outlines the basic features of law in the United States, as law concerns women. By analyzing their legal rights, privileges, and responsibilities, women can better make decisions regarding economic and social problems that are part of everyday life. And by understanding the existing legal framework, women can work to promote changes in social attitudes and legal concepts that will help society to benefit to the full of every individual's potential.

Humankind has always reached out toward the dream of absolute liberty of thought, speech, and action. Both sexes have played an important part in working toward this goal. Yet when men have won a participating voice in government, they have usually insisted on the right to speak for women as well as for themselves.

From the earliest recorded times, society has placed strict restrictions on the legal rights of women. Under the law of Moses, a wife was subordinate to her husband. Daughters could not inherit unless there were no sons. According to Roman law from about the third century B.C., a husband could condemn his wife to death if he thought her guilty of adultery, without even resorting to a trial or a hearing. Later, this law was modified somewhat, but the wife continued to answer to the husband in everything.

Until recent years, women often lived in isolation from the affairs of the world, or even from their communities. Usually they had been given no formal education. They seldom had more than pin money of their own and enjoyed access to few social or organized groups. Women were expected to be entirely absorbed in family and household responsibilities, and they were tied down by the social customs and traditions of the ages. Consequently, women often submitted without question to the male assumption of authority.

Some men feared that granting equality would lead to a lack of control over family life and governmental responsibilities. And for hundreds of years, church leaders spoke with authority, instructing women to stay within the home, the realm supposedly assigned to them by the supreme being's plan for human life. The Bible has frequently been interpreted as assigning women a subordinate position.

The desire for equality was opposed by customs, prejudices, and traditions. Frequently, a woman was "raised to get married" and run a household. Often her functions were limited to child-bearing and housekeeping.

But the fact that progress has been slow does not mean that women—and sometimes men—have not raised their voices in protest. Throughout all history, there has been an undercurrent of demand for legal equality. In his famous book, *The Republic*, written in the fifth century B.C., the Greek political philosopher Plato proposed the education and emancipation of some women. But little actual progress was made for centuries, and women continued to be ignored by lawmakers and educators. Often they remained illiterate; they were not trained to take on important business or professional jobs. Almost without exception, no government allowed a woman to inherit property, make a will, act as a guardian or as an executor of an estate, or serve as an agent for another person. Neither were women permitted to hold important jobs, or vote.

Historians can point to the fact that a few universities in Italy accepted women as students in the fourteenth and fifteenth centuries. But this educational liberation came to an end when there was a change in government in those parts of Italy.

Eventually, England became the cradle of representative government in Europe. In 1499, British women circulated petitions on the street, demanding the right to vote in local elections. These petitions were largely ignored, but they were repeated in a few years. In 1790, Mary Wollstonecraft shocked Britain by publishing *A Vindication of the Rights of Women*, and in 1865, John Stuart Mill unsuccessfully petitioned Parliament to grant women the vote. Early in this century, militant suffragettes demanding voting rights rioted frequently in London, breaking windows and causing extensive property damage. Yet women's right to vote was not granted in England until 1928.

Women did, however, obtain some rights to own real estate at an early date in England. They also obtained the right to make a contract or a will and to sue in court or be sued. Several hundred years ago, Scottish courts granted women the right to testify. But in some parts of England and Wales, property laws continued to limit the right of a woman to inherit real property (real estate) until as late as January 1926.

LIMITATIONS IN THE UNITED STATES

Until about 1795, women in the American colonies were sometimes subject to punishment for speaking out in public. In 1647, Margaret Brent of colonial Maryland publicly demanded a "place and voyce" in the formation of the colonial legislature. Brent was refused this claim. But women property owners in some areas of Virginia were permitted to vote in that colony from 1691 to 1780, when this right was withdrawn. However, it was perhaps not so startling that women were seldom allowed to vote in those early days; only about one-fourth of all male residents could cast a vote in colonial times. The right of suffrage extended only to those who owned substantial property.

In 1775, John Adams, who would become the second president of the United States, was serving as a delegate to the Continental Congress in Philadelphia. Adams was one of the leaders in the formation of a new government as the thirteen colonies approached rebellion against King George III of England. Abigail Adams wrote this letter to her husband John at the time of the Congress:

> I long to hear that you have declared an independency, and, by the way, in the new code of laws, which I suppose it will be necessary for you to make, I desire you would remember the ladies and be more generous and favorable to them than were your ancestors. Do not put such unlimited power into the hands of husbands. Remember all men would be tyrants if they could. If particular care and attention are not paid to the ladies, we are determined to foment a rebellion and will not hold ourselves bound to obey any laws in which we have no voice or representation.

By 1826, property restrictions that had prohibited men from voting had generally been abolished in the United States. Shortly after, Frances Wright, a Scot who had emigrated to America, publicly revived the demand that American women also be allowed to vote, and by the middle of the nineteenth century, the demand for women's suffrage was growing in the United States. Those who worked actively to free the slaves in the Southern states were often also interested in increasing women's rights. In 1848, Lucretia Mott and Elizabeth Cady Stanton organized the first women's rights convention, at Seneca Falls, New York. This meeting was the real beginning of organized agitation for the vote in America. Women circulated petitions, wrote letters, and published articles; in the 1870s, Elizabeth Cady Stanton and other women were arrested for attempting to vote.

Some states granted women voting rights as early as the 1890s, but women's right to vote did not become a reality until August 26, 1920, when the Secretary of State proclaimed the Nineteenth Amendment, giving nationwide suffrage to women, a part of the United States Constitution.

It was only shortly before 1800 that women were generally given the right to a few months' education in public schools in the United States. And it was not until 1819 that the state governments began to recognize that systematic financial aid should be given to the education of both sexes. In a movement beginning in 1848, state laws were passed that permitted women to obtain employment or seek training in the professions.

The last several years have produced considerable legislation of benefit to women. The Fair Labor Standards Act of 1938 and the Equal Pay Act of 1963 insure that women and men who are hired by a company to do identical jobs will get identical pay. Title VII of the Civil Rights Act of 1967 guarantees that people between ages 40 and 64 will not be discriminated against because of age.

Despite these advances, much work needs to be done before women on the job are truly equal to men. According to the Census of 1970, the vast majority of American women earn considerably less than men who work at similar jobs.

LAW AND SOCIAL CHANGE

In examining existing laws that concern women, it may be well to consider some of the social attitudes and conditions under which the legal system operates. Almost from the time of birth, a woman may be encouraged to define herself according to current social customs. The attitudes of relatives, friends, and associates frequently inform young girls that there are certain things a woman cannot do. Girls should not be aggressive; woman's place is in the home. A girl does not need to be told in specific words that society traditionally looks to men for achievement, leadership, and dominance. With this as a backdrop, a woman may be inclined to doubt her ability to compete. Consequently, she may condition herself to pursue a career or other goal in keeping with what society seems to expect of her. Often, no matter what rights and opportunities a woman has, she will decide to pursue the traditional roles her society leads her to desire.

Equal rights for the sexes will never come about by working toward equality in the legal system alone. Changes in social attitudes and conditions must be a necessary accompaniment to laws that place everyone on an equal footing.

We are living in a country with a continuing tradition of liberty and equality, but there are still injustices in American society. And women's success in gaining legal rights has lagged; in many areas, laws govern men and women differently. As we describe some of these differences, the lay reader may be better able to determine what rights she has and whether she needs to turn to an attorney to protect those rights.

chapter 2

Legal Aspects of Marriage

Marriage is, or should be, a freely chosen arrangement that individuals enter into seeking human security, fulfilment, and companionship. The arrangement involves considerable personal commitment between the two people involved. Although it implies certain legal rights and obligations, it is more than an economic scheme to regulate and control property rights; it is more than a mere business deal. There are countless arguments to justify and criticize marriage. But marriage has been the basis of organized society for thousands of years, and likely will continue to be.

Over the years a few isolated court decisions have, in effect, declared that there must first be a sexual consummation of the union before the marriage is legally regarded as actually having taken place. The great majority of the courts, however, have held to the contrary.

Governments have always regulated and defined the requirements and legal rights involved in the marriage relationship. The underlying intent behind this regulation and control of marriage has been to protect the welfare of society, and particularly that of the partners involved and their offspring. Too often, however, the traditional legal safeguards may not measure up to a changing society's needs.

MARITAL RESTRICTIONS IN EARLY LAW

The legal system of the United States is based on that of the British. When the colonies broke away from England in the American Revolution, the Constitution of the new nation included provisions for the creation of a judicial branch of government modeled after the legal principles that had evolved over the years in British courts. So, our modern property laws and laws concerning marriage are based on the old English tradition of law.

Under the laws of early-day England, when a man and woman married they became "one in the eyes of the law." This wording does not imply that husband and wife were equal partners, however. In the social framework of those times, the husband made all family decisions. He had the sole voice in everything concerning money, jobs, or business. He supervised most social affairs and screened invitations. The wife was relegated to raising children and running the kitchen.

From the time of the Norman conquest of England, women were not even permitted to own property without specific approval of the monarch. Women eventually began to win property rights, but for hundreds of years the wife's property was handled by the husband for his sole use during his lifetime. The wife could not legally demand anything, except to be supported by her husband. So complete was the husband's control of the wife's property that there were no legal prohibitions against him selling everything she owned, with or without her will. There was nothing to stop the husband from wasting her money and property, if he saw fit. Farms and other real estate made up most of the wealth of early England. So long as the husband was permitted to control the wife's real estate, he had almost absolute control over everything she owned.

After a time the English courts permitted trusts to be recognized legally. Many of these early trusts were set up so that a bride who owned property could continue to receive rents or earnings from it, even after marriage. This, of course, was a device for bypassing her husband's control. But usually only the well-to-do could afford the expense of setting up a trust.

Even if a woman was allowed to hold a job or to make money in business, some of the old restrictive ideas still continued—until comparatively recent times, a husband was permitted to collect his wife's earnings. Further, in early England there were restrictions that prohibited a wife from testifying in court against her husband, under any circumstances. Some vestiges of this old rule of evidence law can still be traced into comparatively recent times in both England and the United States.

RIGHTS, OBLIGATIONS AND RESPONSIBILITIES

It is obvious that a great many Americans today believe in the benefits and advantages of marriage. Statistics from the 1970s indicate that approximately 97 percent of all women in the United States were either married or would be married at some time. Most people enter into this arrangement with the expectation that it will last throughout life.

The reasons for getting married, of course, vary from couple to couple and from person to person. Most take this step for mutual benefit, to furnish each other with companionship, with sexual gratification, with a prospective family, and with monetary advantages. A man and woman who are in love may not actually discuss these specific considerations during courtship. But all such factors are part and parcel of the marriage contract, arising from state laws and social customs that have the force of law.

Legally, marriage has always been considered a contract that places certain rights and obligations on the two parties. The courts everywhere recognize that the husband has the duty to give financial support to his wife and children, according to his ability. The modern marriage contract obliges the wife to maintain a home for the husband, to care for her mate, to provide for his basic human needs and wants, and to be an acceptable companion. There are some unsettled, gray areas in modern state laws concerning legal obligations when the woman is the breadwinner, if the husband stays home through choice or incapacity. Court decisions vary from state to state. There appears to be a tendency, however, to hold the husband responsible to help where possible with housework and to maintain a proper home when the wife is the sole support.

Legally, however, many courts still take the approach that the wife alone is obligated to perform household services and that her only compensation is the right to her husband's financial support. To grant women equality, the law must look on both marriage partners as being equal in responsibility to the union. Obviously, this is going to require changes in legal interpretations in some areas.

Currently, however, laws that interpret and define the marital relationship have been changing rapidly. Many of these recent changes have placed wives on an equal footing with husbands in some specific legal problems. Nevertheless, there are instances under the law of most states when a woman "ceases to exist when she becomes one with a husband." There are still some situations where only the loss of her husband through death or divorce can actually bring about a complete restoration of individual rights. And again, individual rights for a single woman may be unequal to those for a single man.

All of this may make no difference whatever to some couples. If partners continue to be satisfactorily adjusted in their personal lives, in money matters, and in the many other potential areas of conflict, legal differences may never be in issue. At the same time, it should be pointed out that a legal system merely reflects current social conditions and thinking. Changes in legal decisions or changes in statutory laws, in and of themselves, will not necessarily result in equality. There must be changes in both legal and social attitudes to insure that marriage is a joining of two equals, with neither ever dominated by the other. Psychologists say this is the only satisfactory basis for human trust, love, and mutual growth.

Some of the rights, obligations, and responsibilities of the marriage contract, as it exists in the 1980s, are discussed in the remainder of this chapter.

Who May Legally Marry?

State laws usually prohibit marriages between individuals who are closely related to each other. There is considerable evidence to show that close inbreeding, whether between animals or humans, may result in offspring with health defects and poor mental abilities. There are a great many variances concerning the prohibited relationships in various states. There are also laws on the books in many states that prohibit marriages between people of different races. In addition, practically all jurisdictions place limits on the minimum age of persons who may marry. Individuals below this age may be legally married with parental approval.

Laws in most states permit a woman to marry without consent at an earlier age than a male. Historically, such laws were passed because it was customary for the male to be the breadwinner, and it was thought less likely that he would be able to obtain employment sufficient to support a wife and possible children at a relatively early age.

Some states also require a blood test prior to marraige. A waiting period of several days for obtaining these results is usually necessary. Laws of this kind are designed to make sure that someone with a venereal disease does not transmit it to an unsuspecting marriage partner.

There are other legal restrictions on marriage. For instance, marriages generally may not be contracted between two individuals of the same sex. Your county license bureau can answer any questions about the legality of an intended marriage in your locality.

The Marriage Promise as a Contract

A marriage offer, followed by a proposal, is recognized by the courts as a binding contract. The same general legal rules apply to this situation as to any other contract. If either party backs out of the agreement before the marriage is consummated, the contract has been breached by the withdrawing party.

A generation or two ago it was not uncommon for a woman to sue a man who backed out of an engagement, in a so-called breach of promise suit. In cases of this kind, the "jilted" woman asked for a damage award to compensate for humiliation and for injury to her feelings. In addition, the woman usually asked for damages to compensate for the loss of financial benefits that would have accrued to her as a wife. At times, lawyers played on the sympathy of a jury to obtain extremely heavy money awards from the prospective groom. Almost all of these lawsuits were brought by women.

After a time, some people reached the conclusion that lawsuits of this kind lead to improper abuses. Accordingly, most states passed laws prohibiting so-called heart balm or breach of promise lawsuits. This prohibition is still in effect in most states. There are still a few states, however, where breach of promise suits are permitted, provided the woman is pregnant by the man who backed out of the arrangement. In a few other states, a lawsuit of this kind is permitted, but there are statutory restrictions that limit the amount of damages that may be awarded.

Return of Gifts If an Engagement Is Broken

When a couple goes together, the gifts they exchange are private property belonging to the recipient. This is normally true, whether or not they are engaged. But when a man gives an engagement ring to a woman solely in the expectation that the couple will be married, the majority of courts hold that the ring is his legal property until a wedding occurs. Consequently, it should be returned if the engagement is broken. Not all decisions on this point are in agreement, however. In some cases, the court has permitted the woman to retain the ring if the man broke off the engagement. In one case, the woman was allowed to retain household furniture that had been bought by the man in the contemplation of marriage.

Husband's Obligation to Support Wife and Children

Old English law, which has been followed almost uniformly in the United States, required every husband to support his wife and children. Although this principle has been followed for hundreds of years, the exact amount of support that a husband must provide has never been clearly spelled out by the courts. Generally, the question concerning whether support was adequate in a particular case has been left to the discretion of the trial judge hearing a lawsuit on the matter. The courts do agree quite uniformly that the amount and kind of support furnished must be that reasonably expected under the individual husband's financial ability and standing.

As a practical matter, it is often quite difficult for a wife to obtain a court order to compel her husband to furnish support money for personal needs, so long as she continues to live with her husband. There is a feeling among some judges that the exact amount of support, beyond basic sustenance and a bed, is within the husband's discretion. Consequently, a wife's only recourse may be to file a lawsuit for a divorce or a legal separation.

In one case, a Nebraska judge determined that a stingy husband was providing "adequate" support because he allowed his wife to use a coal-burning stove, had bought her one piece of clothing—a coat—in four years, and had paid for one movie, the only recreation in about ten years! The husband refused to provide an inside toilet or a kitchen sink. But the judge ruled that this support was adequate, even though the husband had a middle-class income and assets worth at least $300,000!

The courts sometimes justify their failure to intervene in the couple's support problems because it would require day-to-day supervision of marital troubles. After a legal separation, annulment, or divorce, the courts will usually step in and fix the exact amount of support money that a man must pay his wife or former wife.

Must a Wife Work?

There are no legal requirements that the wife of an injured or incapacitated husband can be forced to go to work to support the husband. Actually, no one can be compelled to work, except in the case of a convict who is forced to work in a penitentiary. However, the state may require that the wife's assets or salary be used for the destitute husband, if the wife does have assets or income.

Support from Live-In Partners

Generally, unmarried individuals who live together cannot be forced by state or county officials to contribute to each other's support. However, most states do have statutes that require the father of a child born outside marriage to pay reasonable expenses incurred by the mother in connection with the pregnancy and delivery. Thereafter, the father may be compelled to pay for the support of the child, but he is not forced to support the mother outside of marriage. (Child support is discussed in more detail in Chapter 10.)

Duty to Support Offspring

The legal duty to support offspring exists, whether the parents are currently married, divorced, separated, or single. Historically, of course, the duty to support has fallen to the father. But today, the law in almost all states requires both the father and mother to share this responsibility. If the father has disappeared and cannot be located, the mother is very likely to be prosecuted if she flatly refuses to furnish support. Of course, if the mother cannot hold a job, she may be entitled to welfare for both herself and for the child or children.

In some instances there may be a specific court order instructing one of the parents to provide support. In most cases, this order may be an outgrowth of a paternity proceeding, divorce action, or other family matter before the court. A specific court order of this kind takes precedence over the legal obligation on both parents for child support.

In a recent case in the Chicago area, the husband was the sole support of his wife and two small children. He quit his job as a bank clerk and went back to college to obtain a better job in computer science. To survive, the wife applied for welfare for herself and the children. The husband was then prosecuted for nonsupport. During the prosecution of the husband, the judge pointed out that he was completely sympathetic to the husband's desire to improve his job skills. Nevertheless, the judge felt that this commendable objective did not excuse the legal responsibility for support. The husband was placed on probation, since he agreed to resume his old job and go to college part time. Another alternative might have been for the husband to borrow money for family living expenses while going to college full time.

Parental Responsibility for Child Care

The courts of all states uniformly require that a father or mother provide more than mere monetary support for a child. The law specifies that both parents take "proper care" of their offspring. But exactly what is required for "proper care" has never been clearly and finally defined. When the problem has come up, courts have always granted parents wide discretion. Normally, the courts will not interfere with the parent-child relationship unless there is real indication that the child has been starved or physically abused to the point of serious harm or death. It is the parents, not the courts, that have the right to discipline and require obedience. The quality of the home, the clothing furnished, and the nutrition provided are strictly within the discretion of the parent, unless the court decides that parental duties have been badly abused or neglected.

The child's welfare, however, is the first priority of all courts that handle parent-child problems. The parent may be liable under criminal law, but prosecution is rare except in extreme cases. Generally, state and local officials are more concerned with improving the well-being of the child than in prosecuting a parent who may be confused concerning responsibilities. The courts may take a child from the custody of either or both parents if there is evidence that the child is not being given a proper home. Usually this is done, however, only when it becomes necessary for the child's good. (For more information about parent's rights and responsibilities, see Chapter 18.)

Working Wife's Obligations

Marital laws in about half the states still reflect the values of the past, when the husband provided the sole support of a marriage; a working wife has no obligation to support her husband. These states impose no support obligation on the wife even if the husband is ill or completely incapacitated. Ten or more states now provide that a wife must support her spouse from her separate earnings or property when he is unable to support himself through accident or illness. The balance of the states have laws requiring support for the husband, although there are some variances in these requirements.

Husband's Responsibility for Wife's Debts for Necessities

Practically all states permit a wife to charge necessities to her husband if she has been abandoned or if support is not furnished to her. Legal problems sometimes arise as to just what constitutes a "necessity." Most courts would probably refuse to allow charges for extremely fancy groceries, gourmet foods, perfume, jewelry, and other items that are not absolutely essential.

As a practical matter, merchants will usually refuse to extend credit to the account of a husband who has abandoned a wife and children. In some instances, however, a financially sound husband may remain in the community after splitting up with his wife. When this happens, the wife may charge necessary food, clothing, and heating to the husband's account. After charges of this kind have been made, the courts will compel the husband to pay.

In most cases after a separation or divorce has begun, the court will set the amount of support that must be provided by the husband. Usually, the state laws then permit the husband to be free of further debts contracted by the wife for necessities, if the husband places an appropriate notice in the legal notices section of a newspaper. A typical notice of this kind would read:

> Will no longer be responsible for debts of my wife, Lila Grisella Candilla. Signed, Henry Candilla.

By 1979, all fifty states in the United States had adopted the Uniform Reciprocal Enforcement of Support Law. The object of this law is to obtain support money for dependent wives and children in civil proceedings. It is designed to obtain the support money from the individuals who are legally responsible for support and to follow those individuals wherever they may have moved. This legislation applies to:

1. A father responsible for support of offspring up to the age of 21.
2. A husband responsible for support of his wife.
3. A mother legally responsible for support of children under 21 years of age, if the father is incapable, cannot be located, or is deceased.
4. A wife who is responsible for supporting a husband who is unable to support himself and who is likely to become a public charge.

For example, when a husband deserts his wife or family, a state or public agency may be called on to provide assistance. The wife or other person seeking support may be required to go to court in the state of residence and apply for this aid. (Usually a lawyer's services are not necessary in this instance.) If the court determines that the request is valid, support will be ordered. Legal papers are then forwarded to the state in which the breadwinner resides. In most instances, the probation department of the second state attempts to locate the missing husband. Court testimony is then taken in the state where the husband resides, and the husband is given a chance to defend his action or to dispute the claims of his wife. A decision is then made by the court in the first state, concerning whether the husband should be ordered to pay support and/or alimony. This decision is then sent back to the second court to collect money or take other action that will enforce the first court's decision concerning money support or alimony. In some instances, a husband who defies an order of the first court may be imprisoned in the second.

Obviously, a law of this kind would not be needed in a society in which all individuals always lived up to family responsibilities. Cumbersome as it may be, the Uniform Reciprocal Enforcement of Support Act is helpful in many cases. However, it is sometimes impractical to try to make use of this law. A husband may be able to flee and hide his whereabouts, or he may run from place to place whenever discovered, staying away from the operation of the act.

Support for Other Relatives

Whether you have a legal obligation to provide support to relatives other than for a spouse and children varies from state to state. This legal duty also depends on how close your relationship to the person who needs assistance is.

Approximately one-third of the states have no support requirement beyond the marriage partner and children. This is true even if your other relatives and in-laws are unable to work and have neither property nor income.

About two-thirds of the states have laws requiring support of some or all of the following indigents: mother, father, grandmother, grandfather, grandchild, brother, sister, or adult child. You are required to support them if there are no closer relatives who can so provide for them. Under the law in some states, if you do not furnish the required support, county or state officials can sue you for the assistance provided. You may need the help of a local attorney to advise you of your state laws in this responsibility.

Moving into an In-law's Home

A husband cannot compel a wife to move into the home of her in-laws. This is not a "legally adequate" home under the husband's responsibility to provide a home for his wife. If the husband is in such financial difficulty that he cannot provide an adequate separate apartment or dwellling, then some courts would regard the home of the in-laws as adequate on a temporary basis. It is not clear what other courts would hold, but it is believed likely that many judges would feel the in-laws' home is not adequate under any circumstances.

Most courts hold that a wife cannot be forced to accept an in-law into her home at the insistence of her husband. This does not mean, however, that the husband and wife may not be legally liable for the support of an indigent parent of either spouse.

Marital Consortium

The sexual obligations of a wife and husband to each other are legally known as the "marital consortium" or "marriage consortium." This is a duty and a responsibility to each other, and to no one else, during the lifetime of the marriage contract. For hundreds of years, English and American courts have recognized this relationship as a right protected by the legal system, just as the right to possess and use one's own clothes or real estate is protected. If either husband or wife should be injured (incapacitated) by an outsider through negligence or deliberate act, the courts have always allowed the other spouse to sue for "loss of consortium."

In most instances the mate of the injured spouse may recover substantial damages for the "loss of services" of the injured one, even though there may be no loss of income to the couple through the incapacity of a breadwinner. In the past a few courts have regarded the right of consortium as a benefit to be claimed by husbands only. However, today almost all courts permit the claim of loss of consortium as an element of damages in any lawsuit.

The courts usually say that the law implies proper sex relations in every contract of marriage. Continual refusal, without reasonable excuse, is enough to invalidate the marriage if a sexual union never took place. Continued refusal after the marriage has been consummated will often be grounds for divorce. In a case in which a proxy marriage in a foreign country was regarded as valid and legal, an American court held it was not essential that there be subsequent cohabitation in order to complete the marital status.

Lawsuits Between Marriage Partners

Under early English law, neither a husband nor a wife was permitted to sue the other. As noted earlier, the theory of the English courts was that husband and wife were considered one in the eyes of the law. Some old-time judges reasoned that to permit such a lawsuit would "disturb domestic harmony." This prohibition against a suit between marriage partners continued for a long time, even if the husband beat his mate within an inch of her life or the wife struck her husband with an ax.

Approximately half of the states now allow lawsuits between spouses, provided one has wilfully injured the other. However, if the injury arose out of negligence—as a result of an automobile accident, for example—there are fewer states that permit a lawsuit by the injured spouse.

Sometimes the reasoning in an injury situation is that the two spouses could connive together to sue an insurance company, illegally helping the injured spouse to an unjustified recovery of compensation money.

Testimony of One Spouse Against the Other

The courts have long said that private communications between marriage partners are confidential. In practically all states this means that one spouse cannot be forced to testify in court against the other concerning the commission of a crime. If one of the marriage partners has been the victim of a crime perpetrated by the other spouse, however, criminal courts in the United States will now permit this kind of testimony.

The law does not excuse a witness from testifying, however, if the witness merely lived with a person who has been criminally accused. In one case that attracted considerable attention in 1975, a woman was prosecuted for planting and exploding a bomb in a building in which an innocent university researcher was killed. A man who had lived with the accused at the time of the explosion was subpoenaed to testify concerning his knowledge of the bombing. This witness declined to testify, claiming the legal privilege available to a husband and wife. The court refused to extend this right, holding that it was one of the rights and benefits inherent in the marital relationship. The man who refused to testify was jailed for contempt of court.

The court's reasoning here has always been that forced testimony could cause great marital dissention. Rightly or wrongly, courts do not give this privilege in other relationships. Historically, English and

American courts have generally favored bolstering the marriage relationship, rather than favoring those that live together.

Spouse's Responsibility for Crime Committed Wholly by the Other

In early England, a wife was not held criminally reponsible for anything she did on direct orders of her husband. In a case in which a husband ordered his wife to stab someone to death, the husband could be convicted of murder, but the wife who actually did the deed would go free. This decision was reached because of the traditional idea that a marriage was completely dominated by the husband.

Today, whether you are single or married, you cannot be held responsible for a crime committed wholly by someone else. You are, however, solely responsible for your own breaches of the law.

In the early history of English and American law, a married man and wife could not be prosecuted for a criminal conspiracy, since the courts held that the couple was legally *one* and that two or more persons must plot together for a conspiracy to exist. This is no longer the law in most states, where individuals are held criminally responsible for their own acts, married or not.

Property Rights Between Spouses

Property ownership in a marriage can involve a number of legal problems. Many additional problems may also be created if the marriage is broken by divorce or separation. Accordingly, this book contains chapters concerning property ownership and property rights within marriage (Chapter 13) and property ownership and rights when the marriage is terminated (Chapter 10).

Wife's Right to Own Earnings

Around 1850, a series of laws termed Married Women's Property Acts were passed in England and most states in the United States. The general result was to hold that a married woman's earnings are her separate property. (This is considered in more detail in Chapter 13. A married woman's right to contract concerning her separate property is discussed in the same chapter.)

chapter 3

Laws Concerning Your Domicile

WHAT IS A DOMICILE?

The courts define a domicile as the permanent, fixed home of a person who has no intention of moving. Often, an individual's domicile and residence are the same. But sometimes a residence is distinguished from a domicile because the residence is a transient dwelling place (*Fisher* v. *Jordan*, 116F. 2d 183). For example, a college student living away from home may have a residence near the college for four years; but her permanent home—her domicile—is usually her parents' home. Also, a woman who works out of state temporarily may have a residence out of state, but her domicile is legally her husband's permanent home.

The domicile is the place where you maintain your principal residence, as distinguished from a weekend cottage. It is usually said that an individual can have only one domicile at a time. Persons who are traveling may have many residences, but the domicile is the one place that the individual intends to consider as a permanent home.

After a domicile is acquired, a person does not lose it by temporary absences, even if those absences last for several years. For example, an American vice consul in the diplomatic service could live in a foreign country for several years, while retaining a domicile in this country. And like the college student who goes to school out of state, a member of the merchant marine or military service may retain a domicile at the family place of residence.

State laws concerning your domicile may affect your legal rights in a number of ways. The location of your domicile, which is not necessarily the same as your residence, will usually determine:

1. Where you can vote and exercise other political rights, hold public office, and the like.
2. Where you will be subject to state taxes, such as income tax. There are great variances in income taxes from state to state, and obviously it may be advantageous to claim your domicile in a state that has no such tax.
3. Where you may claim lower fees for college or university tuition, fishing and hunting licenses, and so on.
4. Where you may claim property right privileges, such as a homestead exemption.
5. Whether you can sue or be sued in a specific Federal court.
6. Where you may be eligible for welfare or unemployment benefits.
7. Where your will may be probated or your estate administered.
8. Where you may be subject to jury duty, and may obtain licenses such as a driver's license.
9. Which state courts may settle child custody matters and other legal problems.

LEGAL TESTS FOR DOMICILE

If a dispute should arise, the courts usually spell out two legal requirements for establishing a domicile: (1) that it be the place of actual, permanent residence, and (2) that the individual claiming it have the present intention of regarding it as home indefinitely.

The domicile may be changed, if there is a clear intent to change it. The courts may look at any number of factors in deciding whether you have shown an intent to change your domicile. Among these factors, the courts may consider statements you have made to associates about changing the location of your home, whether you have changed your mailing address or have arranged to have mail forwarded, whether you stop paying taxes at the old residence and admit tax liability at the new location, whether you work and bank near the new location, if you get a car license in the new area, and so on.

State laws sometimes confuse the terms *residence* and *domicile.* For example, a statute may specify that "a resident for three years is not required to pay out-of-state tuition at the state university." When a statute of this kind is examined by the courts, they interpret the term "residence" to mean "domicile."

THE OLD LEGAL PRINCIPLE THAT A HUSBAND DETERMINED HIS WIFE'S DOMICILE

According to traditional English and American legal ideas, a man and a woman become a legal unity through marriage. Vestiges of this old idea still remain in many states. Under this principle of legal unity, the husband has the right and responsibility to choose the couple's domicile. At times, this discriminates against the married woman, and in isolated instances it may indirectly work against the husband's individual interests as well. But the husband's right to select the domicile for both marriage partners is still the law in a number of states. A woman may be deprived of her right of domicile by moving away from her husband's domicile.

According to the old English laws, the husband is legally obligated to support his wife and children. Incidental to this obligation to support, the law permitted the husband to choose the domicile. If the husband takes a job in a distant place and the wife refuses to follow, legally she has abandoned her husband. This would be proof of desertion sufficient for a divorce in some states (*Ventrano* v. *Ventrano*, 54 N.Y.S. 2d 537). But the husband must have a good reason to change his domicile. The courts have consistently said that a husband may not acquire a new domicile simply to accuse a wife who stays behind of "deserting" him, in order to divorce her more easily.

For the divorce action to be valid, the wife's failure to follow her husband must be willful and intentional, and without the consent of the abandoned husband. Then too, the courts have said that there are reasonable limitations concerning where a wife might be obligated to follow her husband. For example, a scientist sent to live on the Antarctic ice shelf for a research project could not expect his wife to follow him there.

In states that follow this old abandonment idea (the great majority), the courts hold that a wife may live apart temporarily if she does not intend a permanent separation. Her domicile is still that of her husband. In general, all courts say that a married woman may set up her own separate domicile if she has a reason for a legal separation or a divorce.

Unmarried people have the right to establish their own individual domiciles. So, if a couple is living together, neither partner has a legal right to force the other to move or to determine the other's domicile.

The courts consistently hold that a marriage is valid if it is in accordance with the legal requirements of the place where the ceremony is performed. In some instances, this could mean that a ceremony is valid even though one or both of the partners is considered legally incapable of marriage (because of age or for some other reason) in another state where a domicile is maintained. For instance, a man of 20 and a woman of 17 who maintain domiciles in Utah are too young to marry, according to Utah state law. But if they elope to Nevada, where age limits are less stringent, they can be married legally, and their marriage will be regarded as legal in Utah (the state of domicile) and everywhere else.

If a will is made, the law of the maker's state of domicile controls on questions about the legality of the will's execution, and distribution of the maker's personal property. But if real estate is to pass to an heir under the terms of a will, the will must be executed under the legal requirements in the state where the real property is located.

ESTABLISHING YOUR OWN DOMICILE

There is a definite trend for the courts and some state legislatures to permit a married woman to establish her own domicile. But a number of states lag behind in this area.

A wife can have her own domicile if she wishes to sue someone who lives in another state. In this situation, the law allows her to establish a separate domicile outside of her husband's state of domicile in order to sue in federal court.[1]

Court decisions or state laws in about one-third of the states now permit a married woman to establish a separate domicile, with her husband's consent. In a limited number of other states, a married woman may set up an independent domicile for purposes of running for elective office, for taxation purposes, and for voting and jury duty.[2]

If married women are to continue to make gains in the right to establish a domicile, there must be additional changes in court decisions and state laws, or the passage of a federal constitutional amendment. Where the issue is not completely settled, many lawyers believe that the courts will hold that a married woman may establish her own domicile for all purposes in those states that have enacted equal rights amendments (See Arkansas Statutes Annotated, Sec. 34-1307-1309; Alaska Statutes Annotated, Sec. 25.15.110).

[1]Lawsuits between individuals who live in separate states are judged in Federal court rather than in either state court. This right to sue a person living in another state is guaranteed in the Constitution and is called *diversity jurisdiction* or *diversity of citizenship*. Without this right, the person bringing the lawsuit would be unable to supoena the defendant or reach the defendant's assets at the end of a sucessful suit. In Napletana v. Hillsdale College, 385 Fed. 2d 871, the Federal courts held that a married woman could set up her domicile as different from that of her husband, so that she could qualify for this Federal court jurisdiction. See also Albert Pick & Co. v. Cass-Putnam, 41 Fed. 2d 74.

[2]Leaders in these changes have included Arizona, California, Delaware, Georgia, Indiana, Missouri, Nevada, South Carolina, and Tennessee.

chapter 4

Adoption and Guardianship

ADOPTION PRACTICES

Adoption is voluntarily taking the offspring of another as one's own child. It is the legal procedure that creates the relationship of parent and child between individuals not so related by birth. When the adoption process is completed, the parents and children have the same obligations, rights, and relationships as those of natural parents and children.

Adoption was a feature of ancient Roman law, used with some frequency by wealthy and influential adults who did not have natural heirs to carry on the family name or traditions. However, the old English common law, on which American laws are based, had no provisions whatever for adoption. Until about the middle of the nineteenth century, it was the custom in England to place destitute or homeless children as apprentices. These apprentices learned a trade from the head of the household, assisted a farmer, or worked as scullery maids in the kitchen. In short, the English system treated these children as indentured servants. Those who were not apprenticed were placed in orphanages or lived as street urchins. The plight of these unfortunate youngsters was vividly described by Charles Dickens and other writers. England continued without adoption laws until 1926.

The apprentice system was brought to the United States by early English settlers. But such a system was not suitable to Americans who wanted children of their own. And as settlers came to this country from the mainland of Europe, they brought with them the old Roman legal principles of adoption. Massachusetts passed the first adoption law in 1851, and eventually all the other states legalized adoption. As proof of the acceptance of adoption into our legal system, the distinctions between the rights of adopted and natural children have all but disappeared.

Who Can Be Adopted?

The children who are subject to adoption come from varied family relationships. A husband and wife, alone, may adopt the child or children born to the other mate in a prior marriage. An adoption of this kind may be advantageous to the stepchild, giving the same name and standing to all children under the same roof.

Children born of a marriage are sometimes "put up" for adoption, especially if the family breadwinner is incapacitated or dies. There may simply be insufficient income to keep the family together. In such an instance, a parent may retain some children and place others for adoption. Usually, the courts are reluctant to approve an adoption of this kind unless the reasons appear to be compelling. If the child in question is old enough to understand, the courts will at times refuse to approve the arrangement unless the child consents to it.

The great majority of adopted children are born out of wedlock. In some instances, the mother simply does not want the baby. Or the mother may realize that she is too poor or too young to provide the kind of care that is to the child's best interest. The mother may also reason that her baby will have a better chance for happiness through adoption into a traditional two-parent home. And sometimes the unwed mother feels that a child may interfere with her future opportunities for successful marriage or a career.

American courts have always taken the view that birth out of wedlock is an unfair burden on a blameless child and that adoption will usually offer better prospects to the infant. Therefore, courts almost always favor the adoption of children born outside of marriage, providing the mother is willing.

Consent to Adoption

Laws concerning the consent needed for an adoption vary from state to state. An infant born out of wedlock can never be adopted without the mother's consent, unless the mother is of unsound mind or unless she abandons the baby.

Usually, the father's consent is not needed for an adoption if the child is born out of wedlock. Also, if one of the natural parents is deceased, the consent of the surviving parent is normally sufficient under state law. If the natural parents have been divorced, however, the consent of both is needed, although only one parent may have been awarded custody.

It is not unusual for a natural father to object to an adoption by the mother's new husband following a divorce. The natural father sometimes gives his consent only after the mother and her new husband sign a consent form permitting the natural father to stop making support payments for the child. Regardless of parental consent, an adoption may not be approved under some state laws unless the child also gives approval to the court handling the matter. This, of course, pertains to a child who, the judge feels, is old enough to understand what is taking place.

Basic Legal Adoption Principle

The courts of all fifty states hold that the welfare of the child comes before any other consideration in an adoption procedure. There are, of course, minor differences in the laws and procedures of all states. But in the rules regulating adoptions, the courts are increasingly inclined to set aside or modify procedures that are not believed to be best for the child involved.

STEPS IN THE ADOPTION PROCEDURE

All states have laws concerning how the natural parent's responsibilities and privileges may be severed and how the child may be made a full member of his or her new family. Basically, these laws require the following steps:

1. Securing consent of the child's natural parents in writing. (The father's consent is not necessary if the child was born out of wedlock.) Authorities on adoption problems state that many children remain in foster homes or institutions because parents indefinitely postpone giving consent for adoption. This often occurs in spite of the fact that natural parents cannot or will not provide for the children themselves.
2. Obtaining an application from the individual or individuals who want to adopt.
3. Determining the suitability of the applicant or applicants as adoptive parents. Depending on state laws, this is the responsibility of a state agency or a private adoption agency.
4. Conducting a hearing in which the judge decides the suitability of the new parent or parents.
5. Placing the child in the new home on a trial basis.
6. Issuing a final decree of adoption after a successful trial period. At this time the judge terminates the rights of the natural parents, and a new birth certificate may then be issued in the name of the adoptive parents. Records pertaining to the adoption transactions are then sealed, to be opened only on a court order.

Courts have almost always insisted that adoption procedures remain confidential. Only rarely are spectators allowed. If the adoption takes place when the child is an infant, the identity of the natural parents is usually kept from the growing child, unless the adoptive parents decide to furnish this information. The idea here is to give the child a feeling of identity in the new environment. Of course, in some instances the adoptive parents themselves may not be aware of the identity of the child's natural parents.

Serious consequences sometimes arise if the natural parents learn the whereabouts of their adopted child. There are many instances on record of natural mothers or fathers who have broken into homes where a child had been placed, kidnapping the infant or threatening the adoptive parents. Consequently, the courts that handle adoption matters have long insisted on secrecy.

An additional human and social problem may arise when an adopted child approaches maturity and attempts to establish contact with natural parents. In such a situation an adopted child may be able to convince a court to open adoption records to inspection, if the court can be convinced that the petitioner has enough emotional maturity to handle the problems that may be involved.

The courts with jurisdiction over adoption proceedings vary; sometimes a single state may have more than one court that handles adoptions. It is usually wise for someone who wishes to learn the identity of his or her parents to hire an attorney who can determine what court decided the particular case. At this point you can petition the court to have your records opened; an attorney is not usually necessary for this. But the judge who decides the matter will consider the potential effect on the adoptive child (the petitioner) and the adoptive parents; he or she will investigate the relationship between these parties. In addition, the judge will consider whether the natural mother and father wanted their identities disclosed. The judge will usually need to be persuaded that the petitioner is emotionally mature; an attorney can sometimes help to present a more convincing argument for opening the records.

More often than not, however, adoptees find their searches blocked. The judge in adoption cases has almost complete discretion, and many judges feel that leaving records sealed is the best course in this difficult situation. The natural parents usually gave a child up with the understanding that their privacy would be respected, and any of the parties concerned—including the adoptee—might be hurt by the information revealed. Too often, an adoptee's understandable need to know about forebears results only in frustration and high court costs.

NONAGENCY AND ILLEGAL ADOPTIONS

There has been a continuing demand for adoptable children in the United States since the end of World War II. As a result of this increase, the courts have imposed strict regulations on the procedures to be followed. Typically, these procedures have involved a detailed investigation of the prospective parents, unannounced home visits, and long waiting periods. In a few states today, all adoptions must be handled through state-licensed agencies.

To avoid waiting periods and searching investigations, parents that want to adopt have sometimes become involved in two types of non-agency adoptions—independent and black market. In the independent, or "gray market," adoption, details are worked out directly between the parents concerned. All the necessary papers are signed, and the adopting parents then go to court to obtain the judge's approval. There may be a waiting period before the court makes the adoption final. In an arrangement of this kind, the prospective parents may agree to pay the medical bills of an unwed mother. In a "black market" adoption, a baby is bought and sold. Typically, the mother is a young single woman who left her family or home town to avoid embarrassment. If prospective parents have money and are willing to pay, an infant may be turned over to them immediately.

Gray market adoptions are not illegal; black market adoptions are. In all states it is a crime to buy or sell a baby. Not only may such an act result in a criminal conviction and prosecution, but the courts are very likely to take the child away from the new parents. Lawyers generally agree that prospective parents can legally pay doctor's bills and hospital expenses for the mother, along with attorney's fees. Any payment beyond these items will probably be considered illegal payment for the sale of the child.

RETAINING A LAWYER

Sometimes adoptions are arranged without the help of an attorney. Experience shows, however, that serious problems may arise if the adopting parent or parents do not hire their own attorney. Frequently, adoption agencies retain their own lawyers, but these lawyers are hired to look after the interests of the agency, rather than the problems of the adoptive parents. To protect your own interests, you should have your own lawyer in all adoptions.

REVOCATION OF ADOPTION

Generally, the courts say that adoption is permanent. Once final approval is given by the court supervising the procedure, the adoption can be undone only in unusual circumstances. The judge who presides over this kind of case has wide discretion, however, and can set aside the adoption decree, even years after it was issued, if fraud was involved. For example, if the prospective father covered up a long criminal record, or if the prospective mother was a chronic alcoholic, it is very unlikely that the court would originally have approved these applicants as suitable parents. If these facts later came to light, the court might revoke the adoption.

Under the law in some states, the courts may also revoke an adoption decree if one or both of the parents are jailed as habitual criminals. The adoption decree may also be revoked in a number of states if the parents neglect or abandon the child, if they cannot provide the necessities of life, or if adoptive parents become mentally or physically unable to continue ordinary care.

In some instances, an adoption may be revoked by the judge if both the new parents and natural parents agree that it is best for the child. This occurs rather infrequently, however, and the judge would not take this action without feeling that it was for the child's good.

Often, an unmarried mother gives up her child for adoption and, almost immediately regrets her action. If the mother's consent was given before the child's birth, some states will permit a change of heart after the child is born. But the courts seldom let the mother take the child back because she marries, or becomes able to provide a home, or because her financial condition has improved.

Normally, the courts will not honor the natural mother's request for the return of her child, unless the judge is completely convinced that the child was sold, or that it was taken by outright fraud, misrepresentation, or duress. Situations of this kind occur only infrequently.

WHO MAY ADOPT?

Authorities on adoption say there is no state law anywhere in the United States that specifically forbids a single adult from adopting children. In more than half the states, laws specially provide that "any person" or "any adult" is eligible to be an adoptive parent, and most state statutes ignore any reference to personal criteria. In approximately one-third of the states, there are laws specifically providing that unmarried people are acceptable as adoptive parents.

A number of states do have laws placing restrictions on who may adopt. Several states require the religious faith of the child's natural parents to be matched with that of the adoptive parent, if this does not cause "undue hardship" or if it is "practical." Laws in a few states specify that the child and the adoptive parent must be of the same race. Many lawyers feel that a restriction based on race would be struck down if such a case should reach the United States Supreme Court on appeal.

As a generalization, then, the obstacles to an adoption by a single parent appear to be social rather than legal. Many judges and adoption agency officials feel that a couple can offer a more rounded home life and more attention than a single parent can give. Clearly, this is not always true. A single woman's chance of adoption may turn on her ability to convince the judge that she can furnish a balanced, well-rounded future for the child.

Adoption of Adults

A number of states have laws permitting adults to adopt other adults as their children. Some of these laws require the prospective parent to be from 10 to 15 years older than the person to be adopted. Adoptions of this type are usually designed to make the adopted person eligible for an inheritance, or to carry on the family name. Legal procedures for this kind of adoption require the consent of all parties involved, but no investigation of the parent's suitability is needed.

A WOMAN AS GUARDIAN OR TRUSTEE

In the view of the law, people are not legally capable of asserting their rights, taking care of themselves, or handling their property until they have reached the age of majority. This age varies from state to state, but is usually set at 21.

If an underage child has a father, the father is almost always responsible for handling the minor's legal problems. In a traditional family situation, the law says that the father is the child's natural *legal guardian*. If the father abandons the family or dies, the law automatically regards the mother as the guardian. If the parents are divorced, the court may designate the mother as the guardian in cases when custody is given to the mother.

Parents with minor children may name a relative or friend to serve as a guardian in case both parents should die. The courts will honor a designation of this kind if the parents do die, but if they die without selecting a guardian, the probate court will appoint one. Almost always, this will be an adult who is the nearest of kin. When a guardian is appointed, the legal term for the child involved is *ward*. Law in a few states permit a child of 14 or more to nominate his or her own guardian, and in this situation the courts will usually accept a reasonable designation. But the courts may remove guardians as well as appoint such protectors, if the judge feels that the child's welfare is in question.

It is also common in some states to appoint two guardians for one child—a personal guardian who furnishes personal care and a property guardian who assumes charge of the child's property and money. In some instances, the courts may appoint a separate *guardian ad litem* to look after the interests of a child who is involved in a lawsuit.

Responsibilities and Duties of Guardians and Wards

There is seldom any reason why you should not serve as the guardian of your own child or of a close relative's child. The duties and responsibilities of guardians and wards concerning each other are basically the same as those for parent and child. The expenses of feeding, clothing, and maintaining the ward are taken from the child's own property or money, under supervision of the state court that has jurisdiction. The guardian is not entitled to keep the child's earnings. However, the guardian can recover the expenses and normal payments made in the ward's behalf, including the reasonable value of the guardian's services. This repayment is usually controlled by state laws, with the judge approving the payment of a set fee per month in some states, or by the guardian taking a commission on the amount of money disbursed on the ward's behalf.

Naming a Trustee

If you leave money or property to a minor as a provision in your will, you should name a *trustee* to handle this money or property. This, of course, is because a minor is not allowed to manage his or her own property. There are no legal restrictions concerning the identity of the trustee that you name in this situation, except that the trustee must be an adult of sound mind. The trustee may be a parent, relative, friend, bank, or trust company. If the child receives ownership of property through inheritance, with no will involved, the state probate court appoints a guardian to look after this property.

chapter 5

The Battered Woman

THE WIFE AS VICTIM

Almost any daily newspaper will show that women and men are regularly victimized in murder, mayhem, maiming, assault and battery, and other serious attacks. (Women can also be victims of rape, and Chapter 7 discusses this crime.) Most of these crimes are one-time incidents, but mate beating (assault and battery) may be one of the most frequently repeated crimes in the United States. The purpose of this chapter is to discuss legal aspects of the problem of wife beating, and possible methods that can be used to ward off attacks. Also covered are counseling centers that specialize in the treatment of battered women. The social causes and remedies of this violence are outside the scope of a book of this kind.

OLD LEGAL TRADITIONS GAVE HUSBANDS EXTREME RIGHTS

Traditional English law automatically gave the husband the right to correct, chastise, or discipline his wife, and the wife had no legal right to question or prevent her husband. In this society, the husband was the acknowledged head of the household and his word was law; early law gave him the right to physically punish both wife and children. Legally, this punishment was never supposed to cause injury or be carried to excess; the husband did not have the right to beat or injure a wife. But even if a husband severely beat his spouse, the old English criminal court system offered her little in the way of protection or remedy.

As women's rights have developed, mate beating has become a criminal offense everywhere in the United States. This does not necessarily mean that this kind of violence occurs less often, however (and a few states still have not removed colonial laws that authorize a husband to discipline his wife). In fact, no one really knows how prevalent wife beating is in this country. Police reports and counseling estimates indicate that serious incidents of this kind may occur at least one million times a year. At best this is only an estimate, however, because many, many attacks simply go unreported. But roughly one-eighth of all murders in this country in any given year involve the killing of one spouse by the other.

Wife beating is not to be confused with rough love play, unless serious injury is caused. Legally, the wife is considered to have given consent to all sexual relations with her husband by virtue of marriage, and this consent continues up to a separation or up to the issuance of a final divorce decree (with the law varying from state to state). If the woman is physically harmed, however, the husband can be arrested and tried for assault and battery.

At times, a woman will endure beatings, still feeling some love for her husband and hoping his behavior will change. Some women are simply too afraid, or embarrassed, or uninformed to report these incidents. Other women may live silently with the problem, because wife beating was a fact of life in their own parents' home. A certain number of victims feel trapped by the marriage relationship, knowing that they have no way of making a living if they leave an unreasonable or cruel husband. Unfortunately, experience shows that a husband of this kind will usually repeat his actions, time after time. A woman who is interested in her own safety and that of her children may find it advisable to flee or to exercise some of her other legal options (discussed later in this chapter).

ASSAULT AND BATTERY

The legal name for the crime of beating another person is *assault and battery*. In normal usage, the terms *assault* and *battery* are tied together in American criminal law. When the terms are used individually, we say that an assault is an intentional threat to use force, which would ordinarily cause the threatened individual to believe that there was an immediate danger of serious physical attack. Mere words alone are usually not sufficient to make out an assault, but they will be enough if coupled with some menacing act or threatening gesture. A husband commits an assault when he swings a heavy stick and shouts, "You bitch! I'm going to show you who gives the orders here!"

If the husband goes ahead and uses force, the crime is a battery. An assault, then, is a battery in the making. In actual usage by lawyers and the courts, assault and battery is often used as one term. At times the expression is shortened. So, saying "he committed an assault on her" means that he commenced an assault and it was completed as a battery.

If a husband strikes his wife hard enough to cause "substantial harm"—which can only be defined by a doctor—he can be accused of assault and battery. Assault and battery is, of course, both a criminal act and a civil wrong in all states. The person perpetrating the attack may be prosecuted in criminal court, possibly being sentenced to jail or prison. At the same time, the perpetrator may be sued in a civil court by the victim of the assault and battery. Money damages may be awarded to the victim to compensate for this civil wrong. Both the criminal and the civil court actions may be pursued simultaneously.

Most states have laws that define and classify assaults in various categories, attaching more serious punishments to some. For example, some jurisdictions classify *assault with a deadly weapon* as considerably more serious than a simple assault (such as slapping with the open palm of the hand). Various states also classify some attacks as *aggravated assaults*, *assault with intent to commit robbery*, *assault with intent to commit rape, assault with intent to commit murder,* and so on. (Differences in these various categories are beyond the scope of this book.)

Remedies for Assault and Battery

There is an old saying in the law that "for every legal wrong there is a corresponding legal remedy." But, unfortunately, problems caused by a husband's physical assault on a wife frequently cannot be solved by the legal tools and remedies that are available. Theoretically, these legal remedies will handle the problem. But in actuality, legal remedies may not give the battered wife the help she needs. A wife-beating situation is typically a combination of social, legal, and family problems, affecting both spouses, their children, and their relatives.

As a practical matter, a wife who is beaten should flee immediately if she is able to get away. Where she goes—whether to friends, parents, or to a shelter for battered wives—varies from case to case. A wife who anticipates problems may have alerted a neighbor to call the police at the first sound of trouble. If she is able to, the victim herself should also telephone the police as the first line of defense against violence at home.

Unfortunately, however, police are often reluctant to intervene when they receive "home disturbance" calls. Police officers often say that it is frustrating to handle these problems. Too often, the wife who has called the police turns on the officer who attempts to subdue the husband. In recent years an average of sixteen police officers have been killed every year in the U.S. while trying to break up family fights. Then too, a wife will frequently refuse to sign a complaint after the disturbance has been quieted; often she is frightened of her husband's revenge or hopes that the incident will be forgotten. So police officers sometimes tend to be skeptical of home disturbance calls. Still, calling the police, and if possible fleeing, are the best actions that a woman can take if she anticipates an immediate problem or has been beaten.

Self-Defense

Legally, a wife has the right to use self-defense to ward off physical harm, and in an emergency she is well advised to do so. Law enforcement officials, however, would discourage a woman from relying on self-defense alone to protect herself. If you anticipate violence, you would be wiser to flee.

You always have the right to use reasonable force if you are attacked. State laws vary considerably, however, concerning whether you can use deadly force in defending your person. In most states, any amount of force is permissible if it is completely clear that the assault is so vicious that you could lose your life or suffer great bodily injury. State laws have numerous differences, however. It is possible for a woman to be convicted of murder or manslaughter if she is unable to convince a jury that killing her assailant was the only way she could avoid serious injury or death.

A WIFE'S OPTIONS

Experience shows that some wife beaters will repeat their attacks, time after time, unless the wife flees or outside authority intervenes. The wife whose husband strikes her may have a number of options. Unfortunately, none of them may be completely satisfactory.

Filing Criminal Charges

In most instances, the beaten wife can file assault and battery charges against her husband with state or local prosecuting officials. This process usually begins when the police ask her to sign a complaint after officers respond to her call for help.

From a practical standpoint, however, filing a criminal charge may be a serious mistake. In many instances, the wife's economic future is closely tied to her husband's finances. It will undoubtedly hurt the husband's job prospects if he has a criminal conviction on his record. There are other possible problems, too. In a number of states, matters of this kind are handled in "family court," where the judge may put the husband on probation. This is usually done if the judge feels the husband will straighten up. But if the assault was serious, the judge may send the husband to jail or to prison. This means, of course, that the husband will be out of work and probably will lose his job as a result. In addition, experience shows that a husband often greatly resents being sent to jail, and when released he may return to beat his wife more severely than ever. If the wife should obtain a divorce, the husband may be unable to pay alimony or child support if he is jailed.

If the wife believes it is in her best interest to prosecute, she should help make the prosecutor's case. A police report should be filed immediately. Scars or marks should be photographed and the photographs placed in police files. The wife should insist on a medical examination to establish the extent of injury. Neighbors or others who could serve as witnesses should be identified, and their names and addresses should be made available to police investigators.

A police official described the difficulties of the typical situation with respect to prosecution:

> It's the victims themselves who make the felony crime of wife-battery difficult to enforce. We go out on at least one felony wife-battery call a day. And we try our best to prosecute. But a lot of women won't go through with it. They're afraid to prosecute, to sign a complaint a lot of the time.
>
> It's hard for some of them to realize that they have to help us if they want us to help them . . . The main thing is to condition the women . . . to learn that they have to prosecute to do something about it.[1]

Police point out that wife beating follows a fairly continuous cycle of violence and that the violence usually continues, rather than diminishes.

Suing the Husband in Civil Court

Until comparatively recent times, a wife could not sue her husband because of the old legal principle that "a husband and a wife are legally one." This rule was based on the idea that the courts should never disturb the marital relationship. But a wife who is beaten seriously should ask herself if she has a relationship worth keeping.

As a practical matter, lawyers sometimes discourage filing a lawsuit of this kind, unless the husband has considerable money or property. Otherwise, the lawsuit may not result in much for the wife—

[1]Detective Sgt. Joe Thompson, General Investigative Section, Long Beach, California, Police Department, Long Beach *Independent, Press-Telegram*, July 20, 1980, p. L/S6.

except a bill from her lawyer. Then too, such a suit is not likely to be settled for months.

If a suit is filed, various states have various laws that may apply. Some state laws differentiate between the wife's right to sue her husband for bodily harm, to sue for negligence, or to recover for character injuries her husband causes. More than half the states only allow a wife to recover for beatings in a lawsuit, or to recover for other bodily injuries caused by the husband's negligence. Some states restrict assault lawsuits to a so-called family court or domestic relations court. Some will permit lawsuits for deliberate physical injuries by the husband, but limit lawsuits in case of the husband's negligence to injuries resulting from an automobile accident. A few states will not allow a wife to recover damages against her husband, even if he commits a brutal assault or causes harm through his negligence. Nevada currently does not have any law that touches on lawsuits between the spouses.

Vacate Orders, Cease and Desist Orders, Peace Bonds

In many states, a judge can issue a Vacate Order to keep a violent husband out of the family residence. If the husband goes to the home, he may be thrown in jail for contempt of court. In some instances, a judge may issue a Cease and Desist Order, or a Restraining Order as it is sometimes called. This usually specifies that the husband stay out of the home, or that he refrain from approaching within a specific distance of his wife until the matter is settled by a divorce or other appropriate action.

In other cases, the judge may require the husband to be brought into court for a hearing. At that time the judge will ask the husband to promise that he will not molest his wife or family. The judge may then require the husband to post a Peace Bond. Any effort toward annoying the wife results in forfeiture of the bond, with the money represented by the bond being forfeited to the court.

COUNSELING, SHELTERS, DIVORCE

Knowlegeable marriage consultants point out that there are a number of counseling centers available to help spouses who have been involved in beating incidents. Some help in this regard is usually available through church organizations or family court officials, as well as through established social agencies.

The National Organization for Woman (NOW) has been a leader in offering advice, counseling, and shelter to battered wives. The national headquarters is located at 1957 East 73rd Street, Chicago, Illinois 60649. Local chapters of this organization offer help in major metropolitan areas.

There may be a noticeable increase in shelter facilities available to victims of wife beatings in the near future. This is an especially valuable resource for a wife who has no career or job training and who therefore feels it would be disadvantageous to obtain a divorce.

Some marriage counselors advise a battered wife to divorce her husband immediately, before the family has children. These counselors point out that, if beatings continue, the wife's problems may be much greater after the arrival of children and that it may be necessary for her to make trip after trip to a shelter.

Shelters typically seek to obtain newspaper publicity so that battered wives will know of their availability. Although the telephone number of the shelter is given publicity, the shelter's location is kept strictly confidential. Police officials who work with wife-battery problems will frequently escort a victimized wife and children to the nearest available shelter.

Organization for Husbands

Some violence-prone husbands, admitting the reality of their illness, may join an organization such as Alternatives To Violence. Other husbands may be required to attend meetings of this kind or instructions from a family court judge. Experience shows that those who voluntarily join together may learn to control their problem, but the success rate for husbands who are forced to attend is usually low.

chapter 6

Abortion, Birth Control, and Sterilization

ABORTION

There has never been any legal prohibition against the right to have children in English or American law. But the reverse of this problem, the right not to have children, has given rise to bitter legal disputes. Almost any woman feels that she should be free to make and carry out a number of personal choices that will affect her own life. For many women, one of these basic choices involves the right to bear children or to remain childless. However, no contraceptive device or technique except sterilization or vasectomy is completely dependable. So, when an unwanted pregnancy occurs, women often turn to abortion.

Unwanted births affect not only the individual mother, but other members of her immediate family. In many instances, unwanted children are a burden, not only to their parents, but to society and the state and all the state's resources. Then too, unwanted, disadvantaged children may be born into a world of constant hardship and misery.

What is Abortion?

In the case of *McClure* v. *State*, 215 SW 2d 524, abortion was defined as:

> The intentional expulsion of a fetus from a woman before it is capable of carrying on its own life.

Black's Law Dictionary defines it as:

> The expulsion of the foetus at a period . . .so early that it has not acquired the power of sustaining an independent life.

The legal term *procuring miscarriage* is sometimes used interchangeably with the term *abortion* (*People* v. *Rankin*, 74 P. 2d 71, 10 Cal. 2d 198).

Modern Abortion Laws

In early England, Catholic Church authorities and some representatives of the Church of England said that abortion was no moral or legal violation until the fetus was formed and had acquired a soul. This point was "fixed" by church officials at 40 days for a male and 80 days for a female! Under the old common law of England, abortion was a crime if it occurred after "quickening," the time at which there are recognizable signs of movement within the mother. This usually takes place about the end of the sixteenth week of pregnancy. After this time, an induced miscarriage was a crime. In 1803, England adopted an antiabortion law called Lord Ellenborough's Act, which made deliberate expulsion of the fetus a violation if the woman "was quick with child." Beginning with New York in 1828, a number of states in the United States passed laws along the general lines of the English act. After a time, the distinction between a quickened and an unquickened fetus began to disappear, and state laws made abortion a crime at any stage of pregnancy.

But women who are desperate enough will obtain abortions—whether or not they are legal. Contrary to the protests of some groups, laws against abortion will not always save the lives of unborn children and will often endanger the lives of pregnant women who turn to unlicensed, illegal abortionists.

In recent years there has been a great wave of feeling, especially in the United States, that a woman should have the right to do what she wants to with her life. Thus, she should have the right to determine whether she wants to marry and whether she wants to have children. If she should become pregnant without intending to, many now feel that she should have the right to a medically safe, legal abortion. Polls taken throughout the United States in 1979 and 1980 revealed that approximately 80 percent of adults believe that every woman should have a choice concerning an abortion. At the same time, highly vocal, well-organized opposition to any kind of abortion has developed, generally through church-related "right to life" organizations.

The legal question of abortion can be expected to be highly controversial, perhaps even for years to come. As Justice Blackmun of the United States Supreme Court pointed out in 1973, there is an awareness of the sensitive and emotional nature of the abortion controversy, of the vigorous opposing views, even among physicians, and of the deep and seemingly absolute convictions that the subject inspires. One's philosophy, one's experiences, one's exposure to the raw edges of human existence, one's religious training, one's attitudes toward life and family and their values, and the moral standards one establishes and seeks to observe are all likely to influence and to color one's thinking and conclusions about abortions.

At any rate, in 1973 the Supreme Court of the United States decided to consider the question of the right to an abortion. Two cases were heard simultaneously, the Texas case[1] of *Roe* v. *Wade*, 410 U.S. 113, and a companion case, *Doe* v. *Bolton*, 410 U.S. 179, an appeal from Georgia. Both cases involved substantially the same constitutional questions.

In these two cases, the Supreme Court refused to decide that a woman has an absolute right to an abortion under all circumstances. The court did hold, however, that the near-century-old Texas statute was unconstitutional because it violated Jan Roe's right to personal

[1]The Texas statute that was in dispute was similar to others, such as: Ariz Rev Stat Ann Sec. 13-211 (1956); Conn Pub Act No. 1 (May 1972 special session) (in 4 Conn Leg Serv 677 (1972), and Conn Gen Stat Rev Sec. 53-29, 53-30 (1968) (or unborn child); Idaho Code Sec. 18-601 (1948); Ill Rev Stat, c 38, Sec. 23-1 (1971); Ind Code Sec. 35-1-58-1 (1971); Iowa Code Sec. 701.1 (1971); Ky Rev Stat Sec. 436.020 (1962); La Rev Stat Sec. 37:1285 (6) (1964) (loss of medical license) (but see Sec. 14-87 (Supp 1972) containing no exception for the life of the mother under the criminal statute); Me Rev Stat Ann, Tit 17, Sec. 51 (1964); Mass Gen Laws Ann, c 272, Sec 19 (1970).

privacy. The court pointed out that laws should not infringe upon the rights of a woman and her doctor to decide whether she should have an abortion at an early stage of pregnancy. However, since an abortion is more dangerous after the first three months, the court then added that the state does have a legitimate and important interest in safeguarding the health of a pregnant woman. As the pregnancy continued, it could be a foolhardy thing for a woman to insist on an abortion. Based on available medical knowledge, the Supreme Court said that after the first three months of pregnancy the state's interest could come into play. The court continued that after this three-month period, the state could, if it chose to, place restrictions on abortions, designed to: (1) protect the pregnant woman's health by making abortion illegal after the time when risks to the woman have substantially increased, and (2) protect the interest in potential human life, unless an abortion appears necessary to the preservation of life or health of the mother.

Rights of the Single Woman

Doe v. *Bolton* concerned abortion for a married woman. But in *Roe* v. *Wade*, the woman seeking an abortion was single. The Supreme Court's decision in the Roe case said in effect that a single woman has as much right to an abortion as a married one. In this position, the court seemed to be relying on its prior decision in *Eisenstadt* v. *Baird*, 405 U.S. 438, in which the court indicated that there were no substantial differences in the constitutional rights of married and single people.

Requirement of Parental Consent

The Roe and Bolton cases did not decide all the troublesome problems of abortion. In the 1976 case of *Planned Parenthood Assn.* v. *Danforth* the Supreme Court held unconstitutional a Missouri law requiring a minor to have parental permission for an abortion. The court's opinion in this instance was:

> Constitutional rights do not mature and come into being magically only when one attains the state-defined age of majority. Minors, as well as adults are protected by the Constitution and possess Constitutional rights. (44 United States Law Week 5197 at page 5204, Docket Nos. 74–1151 and 74–1419).

The Supreme Court implied that this decision did not hold that all state laws insisting on parental approval would necessarily be held unconstitutional. In clarification, the court said that a state statute would be proper if it gave the pregnant minor the chance to obtain a court order for an abortion that would override a requirement of prior parental approval (*Belotti* v. *Baird*, 44 United States Law Week 5221, Docket Nos. 75–73 and 75–109).

Right to Privacy

Whether a woman having an abortion has a right to insist that such records remain confidential has never been decided by the United States Supreme Court. In a Utah case in 1973, the federal courts ruled that a state law that subjected an abortion decision to public scrutiny by making details of every abortion a matter of public record violated a woman's right of privacy (*Doe* v. *Rampton*, 366 F. Supp. 189).

Consent of Father

Following the court's decision in *Roe* v. *Wade*, a number of states passed laws requiring the father's consent to an abortion. These laws imposed one of three wordings on this restriction: (1) that the husband of a minor wife was required to approve, (2) that the husband of the pregnant woman had to consent, or (3) that the father of the fetus had to approve. In *Planned Parenthood* v. *Danforth*, already discussed, the Supreme Court said, in effect, that the right to an abortion was the woman's right alone, although the father, of course, always has an interest.

In *Doe* v. *Bellin Memorial Hospital*, 479 F. 2nd 756, a hospital rule requiring the father's approval before an abortion would be performed was held to be improper. The court said that the right to an abortion is the woman's right, and that requiring the medical profession to observe unnecessarily abortion-restricting rules is invalid. However, the court here pointed out that the hospital in this case was one receiving Federal funds for conducting abortions. The court noted that a private hospital, operating on private funds, could set its own rules for the way in which abortions could be performed.

Similarly, the Florida courts held that the father of a fetus did not have the right to a court injunction prohibiting the mother from obtaining an abortion. The court reached this holding, even though the father was ready and willing to marry the mother and give support and care to the child (*Jones* v. *Smith*, 278 So. 2d 339).

Abortions Under Reasonable Medical Conditions

All decisions of the United States Supreme Court and appropriate state courts have consistently inferred or actually stated that the individual states have the right to pass laws requiring reasonable safeguards and precautions for the safety of the woman involved. This means that any state could prohibit abortions performed by untrained individuals or conducted in unsanitary or unsafe places.

In mid-1980, the Supreme Court reaffirmed the decision in *Roe* v. *Wade*, that a woman has a right to an abortion under medically adequate standards and within the first three months of pregnancy. At stake, however, was the right to Federal funding of abortions by women in need. The court upheld the constitutionality of the so-called Hyde Amendment, which forbids all but a few federally funded abortions.[2] At the same time, the Supreme Court left free the possibility that individual states would pay for abortions for the needy. As a practical matter, however, it does not appear likely that state governments will be inclined to absorb such costs.

A good many people feel, however, that a right is hardly a right unless it can be utilized by those who need it. And without federal funding, poor women often learn that the right becomes meaningless. The solution for the future may be to induce Congress to pass laws specifically funding abortions in those instances where they are needed.

Abortion Refusal

If you are refused an abortion, there are a variety of sources that can offer legal help or suggest other hospitals that will perform the operation legally. Planned Parenthood, the American Civil Liberties

[2]Details about the so-called Hyde Amendment are not of further interest concerning the legality of abortions.

Union, NOW, or Legal Aid can be of help and are usually listed in the phone books of large cities. The National Abortion Rights Action League has its headquarters in Washington, D.C. and has local offices in metropolitan areas.

CONTRACEPTIVES

In 1961, Estelle T. Griswold, Executive Director of the Planned Parenthood League of Connecticut, set up a family counseling and operating center at New Haven, Connecticut. With a professor at Yale Medical School, Griswold gave instructions, information, and medical advice to married people concerning the means of preventing contraception. Griswold was convicted in state court of violating Connecticut state statutes, which made the use of contraceptives a criminal offense and which set criminal penalties (*Griswold* v. *Connecticut* 381 U.S. 479 and General Statutes of Connecticut [1958 Rev.] Sections 53–32, 54–196).

> Any person who uses any drug, medicinal article or instrument for the purpose of preventing conception shall be fined not less than fifty dollars or imprisoned not less than sixty days nor more than one year or be both fined and imprisoned . . . and
>
> Any person who assists, abets, counsels, causes, hires or commands another to commit any offense may be prosecuted and punished as if he were the principal offender.

Griswold and others were convicted and fined $100 each. The matter was then taken to the United States Supreme Court on appeal. In 1965, the Supreme Court held that a state law prohibiting the education in contraceptives or use of contraceptives by married people is unconstitutional.

After delivering a lecture on overpopulation and contraception, William R. Baird invited members of the audience to come to the stage and to help themselves to contraceptive articles, and he personally handed a package of contraceptive foam to a young woman. As a result of giving the foam to the woman, Baird was convicted in a Massachuetts state court for violating a state statute that made it a crime to sell, lend, or give away any contraceptive drug, medicine, instrument, or article, except that physicians were permitted to administer or prescribe contraceptive drugs or articles for married persons, and pharmacists were permitted to fill prescriptions for contraceptive drugs or articles for married persons.

Following conviction, this case (*Eisenstadt* v. *Baird*) was appealed to the United States Supreme Court. In 1972, the Court held that state law could not prohibit the sale or use of contraceptives by unmarried individuals.

A Minor's Right to Contraceptives

An old New York law made it a criminal violation to sell or distribute nonprescription contraceptives to individuals under 16 years of age. It was legal, however, for such contraceptives to be dispensed by a doctor. In a test of this law, a Federal court held that it was unconstitutional, since it violated the Fourteenth Amendment of the United States Constitution. This case (*Population Services International* v. *Wilson*, 383 F. Supp. 543) did not reach the Supreme Court, however, and there is a difference of opinion concerning whether minors actually have a right to buy contraceptives. Planned Parenthood can offer advice for your area.

STERILIZATION

Sterilization is any physical or surgical procedure that makes a person incapable of sexual reproduction. This does not mean, of course, that the procedure will have any effect on sexual capacity or functions.

Beginning in 1907, a number of states in the United States passed laws that provided for compulsory sterilization of certain people who were confined in state mental institutions. At least 32 states and Puerto Rico eventually passed laws of this type. Most of these enactments provide that the state may sterilize institutional inmates in cases of idiocy or severe feeblemindedness, gross physical defects, and general hereditary conditions that are considered certain to be transmitted to offspring. Some other laws of this kind provide for sterilization of individuals convicted a number of times for criminal rape or for other repeated convictions of serious crimes.

In *Buck* v. *Bell,* 274 U.S. 200, the first matter of this kind reached the United States Supreme Court on appeal. The case involved a woman who was the daughter of an imbecile. This daughter, herself an inmate of a state mental institution, was also considered hopeless by a number of medical doctors. State authorities wanted to sterilize the daughter after she had given birth to a third-generation imbecile. Justice Holmes, speaking for the majority, held that the state statute authorizing sterilization was constitutional and proper. In this opinion, Justice Holmes said:

> We have seen more than once that the public welfare may call upon our best citizens for their lives. It would be strange if we could not call upon those who already sap the strength of the state . . . society can prevent those who are manifestly unfit from continuing their kind . . . Three generations of idiots are enough. . . .

The constitutionality of a state statute authorizing sterilization was again upheld in the case of *In Re Simpson,* 180 N.E. 2nd 206. In yet another leading case on sterilization, *In Re Hendrickson,* 123 P. 2nd 322, the Washington State Supreme Court upheld the constitutionality of a state law giving authorities the right to sterilize certain types of individuals being held in state institutions. In the same decision, however, the court held that sterilization could not be permitted in the case under consideration. This was because state officials had not given adequate hearings to the person to be sterilized, along with an adequate opportunity to show that sterilization was proper in that instance.

Legal authorities can only surmise concerning the legality of sterilization. It is believed that courts will probably continue to uphold the state's right to sterilize, but only after giving adequate hearings to those involved.

In recent years, some individuals have proposed compulsory sterilization for mothers who want to remain permanently on welfare. Proposals of this kind have been strongly denounced by civil rights groups. It seems unlikely that this kind of sterilization would be permitted to become law or be upheld as proper by the courts. Matters of this kind will come under increasing legal scrutiny in the future.

chapter 7

What To Do about Rape

RAPE

From the earliest times in the English system on which our law is based, rape was considered one of the most serious of all crimes. For many years the death penalty was uniformly imposed. In the United States, rape is a felony in all jurisdictions. The penalties imposed usually vary from imprisonment for one year to a life sentence. In extreme cases, the death penalty applies in some states.

The crime of rape always originates in and includes the crime of assault. If the attack continues until sexual penetration, the crime is rape.

To the thinking of some, rape is a crime of uncontrolled sexual passion. According to this thinking, a woman who is raped is sometimes made to feel that she caused the attack by wearing provocative clothing, walking the streets at night, or whatever. But criminologists who study the problem often feel that rape is basically a crime of violence, not a crime of passion. They have come to believe that a rapist usually attacks because of deeply aggressive hostility to women, not because of sexual excitement. Certainly it is true that rapists do not limit their attacks to young or conventionally attractive women. Girls and women of all ages have been raped.

In general, judges and police personnel are becoming more sympathetic to the rape victim's situation. But, of course, there are still people who feel that the victim somehow "asked for it."

RAPE DEFINED

Generally when we use the term *rape*, we are speaking of so-called *common law rape* or *forcible rape*. Under the law of most states, rape is defined as:

> An act of sexual intercourse by a male with a woman other than his wife in which the woman resists and her resistance is overcome by force or great fear. Any sexual penetration, however slight, is sufficient to complete the crime. Generally, both resistance and force are required. If the perpetrator uses a weapon or threatens great bodily harm without exerting force, the courts usually say the woman need not cry out or resist, if it appears serious harm is imminent. Rape is distinguished from seduction in that the former requires force or a serious threat, while in seduction the woman is persuaded to participate. If the woman consents in the end, the crime is not rape, even though force may be used at the outset. When the woman is unconscious, drugged, mentally ill, or so intoxicated that she does not know what she is doing, the courts say that she is incapable of giving consent, and the offense is rape.[1]

The courts in most states also recognize that rape may be committed by fraud rather than through the use of force (from the California Penal Code, Sec. 261). Generally, this kind of rape falls into one of three basic situations:[2]

1. A "pretend" doctor or medical doctor orders the victim to engage in intercourse under the claim that it is a necessary medical treatment.

[1]Charles F. Hemphill and Phyllis D. Hemphill, *Dictionary of Practical Law*, Englewood Cliffs, N.J.: Prentice-Hall, Inc. 1979, 176; Smith v. Superior Court, 295 P. 2d 982.

[2]Allen Z. Gammage and Charles F. Hemphill, Jr., *Basic Criminal Law*, 2nd ed., New York: McGraw-Hill, 1979, pp. 189, 190.

2. An impersonator of her husband gets into bed with the victim when it is dark, or when the victim is asleep.
3. A man goes through a mock wedding ceremony and engages in sexual intercourse with a woman after inducing her to believe that she is legally married to him (Mooney v. State, 15 S.W. 724).

RESISTANCE AND FORCE

Early court cases held that a rape conviction could not be sustained unless the victim had resisted to the utmost of her ability (*People* v. *Carey*, 119 N.E. 83). Later court decisions modified this requirement somewhat, saying that there must always be genuine resistance, but that it must be appropriate to the circumstances of each case. If the attacker held a gun at a woman's throat and seemed ready to use it, the courts held that further resistance would be futile. But the court decisions have never done away with the requirement of legitimate resistance, holding that "mere verbal disapproval" by the victim is insufficient (*Culbert* v. *State*, 129 So. 315).

Occasionally, a case occurs in which a woman offers considerable resistance at the outset, but does not continue to oppose her attacker. In one such case, the evidence was clear that the woman offered initial resistance; however, the evidence disclosed that the physical contact aroused her so much that she did not oppose the intercourse at the time the penetration was actually made. Since the legal test for rape is that the victim never gives consent, the court said that no crime occurred (*Wade* v. *State*, 138 S.E. 921).

In one case, a woman was kidnapped by six robust men and dragged away. She offered great resistance when one of the men raped her, but she did not fight against any of the other five who forced sex on her. The court said that it was obvious to her that further struggle would have been futile. The court convicted all of her attackers, in spite of the claims by one of the accused that she had not resisted him (*Salerno* v. *State*, 75 N.W. 2nd 362).

Lack of Consent

The courts consistently hold that sexual intercourse with the woman's consent is not rape,unless she is legally incapable of giving her consent. If the woman is so intoxicated that she does not know what she is doing, is drugged, or is mentally ill, the law says that she has not given her consent. Consequently, the act would constitute rape. In some cases, a woman has been sexually attacked while anesthetized or after fainting. Here again, the courts hold that she has been raped, since she cannot give consent (*Lancaster* v. *State*, 148 S.E. 139).

In seeking to determine whether the woman consented, the courts usually determine whether the victim made whatever outcry was possible. Courts regard crying out or screaming with a loud voice as extremely strong evidence of refusal to consent. But if the woman does not cry out because she fears her cries will result in her immediate death, then it is not necessary for her to have screamed (*People* v. *Silva*, 89 N.E. 2nd 800).

Force–Used or Exhibited

The court decisions consistently say that the victim's resistance must always be overcome by force, or by genuine fear that present, impending force will do the victim great bodily harm or result in death. If a woman is knocked unconscious with a club, obviously force was used. Further decisions point out that there is no specific minimum amount of force against which resistance is always necessary, unless the male uses a weapon or otherwise causes the woman to believe she will be seriously harmed by resisting. Bruises, marks of violence, scratches, blood, torn clothing, overturned furniture, and smashed personal articles are among the evidence that the prosecution may use to prove that the accused actually used force.

CATEGORIES OF RAPE

Rape by the Husband

Under the definition of rape generally used by the courts, we noted that the crime as "an act of sexual intercourse by a male with a woman other than his wife." According to this commonly accepted definition, in most states it is not legally possible for a husband to rape his own wife. This rule is based on the old English common law concept of the husband and wife being legally one. As one early-day English legal scholar (Sir Matthew Hale, 2 Bish. Crim. Law 1135) summarized the wife's legal position: "In marriage she hath given up her body to her husband."

When English criminal law was brought to America, the courts continued to interpret cases according to this rule. As one American judge put it: "One of the legal presumptions of marriage is that the wife has given her consent to all sexual relations." Another early American judge deciding such a case said that "Courts usually do not go behind the domestic curtain and scrutinize too closely every family disturbance, even though amounting to an assault . . . "(*State* v. *Dowell*, 11 S.E. 525).

Of course, in extreme cases the courts have found the husband guilty of rape. For example, one husband was convicted of attempted rape after the evidence showed that he held his wife and another man at gunpoint, ordering the second man to have sexual relations with his wife. The attempt failed because the second man was so terrorized that he was unable to perform (*State* v. *Dowell*, 11 S.E. 525). And in an early Missouri case, the court had no difficulty in finding an ex-husband guilty of rape in a sexual assault on his nonconsenting, divorced wife (*State* v. *Parsons*, 285 S.W. 412).

But under the existing law in more than one-half the states in this country, a husband can still never be prosecuted for rape until the divorce becomes final. This is so even if the husband sexually attacks the wife after she has moved out and has started divorce proceedings. In most instances, all that can be done in such a situation from a prosecution standpoint is to bring an assault charge.

Beginning in 1967, a number of states began to pass laws designed to correct this judicial deficiency. Most of these laws now permit the wife to file rape charges against the husband if the spouses are living apart or are legally separated. The terms of these laws vary somewhat from state to state. Obviously, additional legislation is needed in a number of states, making the sexual assault of a wife who is living apart from her spouse a rape violation.

In recent years a wife in Oregon filed a rape charge against her estranged husband. The matter received considerable newspaper publicity. The husband was acquitted in a jury trial, and the wife and husband were reconciled shortly thereafter. Some newspaper accounts wrongfully interpreted this judgment to mean that a husband could still not be convicted for raping his wife. In fact, it meant only that the husband was acquitted in that particular case.

Although prosecutions of husbands have been rare, many women feel that the time has come when the law should no longer assume that a woman must be completely subject to her husband's will.

Consequently, the fact that a couple is living together should not justify a brutal sexual assault against an unwilling wife. Acting under this logic, a number of groups throughout the United States are currently working for legislation to make every husband criminally responsible for a violent sexual assault, even if he is living with his wife at the time the attack takes place. Whether statutes of this kind will be passed into law in all states is a matter of conjecture.

Rape by Man Living with Woman

When a man and woman live together outside of marriage, most courts treat them as if they were legally married for purposes of this situation, refusing to recognize the possibility of rape. Generally, the only prosecution action available is to file an assault charge.

Other Activities Designated as Rape

Exactly what activities constitute rape vary considerably from state to state. In a few jurisdictions, the crime of rape does not include *sodomy*. Here again, definitions vary from state to state, with sodomy usually being defined as sexual contact with any body cavity other than the vagina. Most jurisdictions classify sodomy as a separate crime.

Under the usual definition of rape, a man cannot be the victim of the crime. However, rape laws in some states include forced homosexual activity with a male victim.

Almost all states have a number of laws that prohibit certain kinds of sexual activity. For example, if an impotent man sexually assaults a woman with a screwdriver, the state law may classify such conduct as an aggravated sexual assault.

Statutory Rape

Statutory rape occurs when a man has sexual intercourse with a consenting female who is under the age specified by state law. This age, called the "age of consent," varies between 10 and 18 in different states. Criminal prohibitions against statutory rape protect girls of tender years by making it the male's responsibility to be sure of the girl's age prior to having sexual relations. Most courts say that the law presumes, without exceptions, that a girl under the statutory age does not have sufficient experience or knowledge of human problems to understand or judge the emotional, social, moral, or physical consequences of a sexual relationship.

IF RAPE OCCURS

If you are raped, try to remain as calm as possible and use your own intelligence to do what you must to escape or survive. Law enforcement officers feel that there is no one best course of action. In some cases, it is wise to scream or to blow a whistle; the noise may frighten the rapist or summon help. In other cases, especially if the rapist is armed or threatens violence, it is sometimes best not to scream. The same advice applies to resisting the rapist. Women have been known to frighten off potential attackers, or even to capture them, but sometimes a violent rapist injures or kills a woman who resists. Whether to fight back is a decision you must make at the moment of attack. Much in your decision may depend on the particular situation you are in. But self-defense classes can be a valuable tool for women who wish to build confidence and resist an attacker.

Call the police as soon as you feel it is safe to do so. They may be able to capture the rapist quickly, near the scene. And, unfortunately, any delay in reporting a rape may lead a jury to question your testimony.

If at all possible, get a sympathetic friend or relative to stay with you or call a rape hotline if one exists in your area. Sometimes a member of the staff will immediately come to your aid. Usually, the police will let your friend stay with you during questioning and examination, although you do not have a legal right to demand a friend's presence.

Helping Conviction

Conviction is one of the most effective deterrents to rape, especially since many rapists repeat the crime if they are not caught. In most instances, the prosecutor's case against the attacker can be greatly assisted if the victim recalls specifics about the criminal. Obviously, if you are raped, helping a prosecutor get a conviction is not the first thing on your mind. But if you can avoid panicking, you may be able to summon assistance, or at least remember enough about the rapist to convict him—so he will not strike again.

If the risk appears to be worth taking, you may summon assistance or alert possible witnesses by loudly calling out for help. This may also frighten the rapist away. Calling out may turn someone's attention to the rapist, his car, his dress, or to other details that may help police to identify him. The fact that you called out may also erase any doubt in a jury's mind as to whether the attack was genuine.

Sometimes women obtain evidence for the police. Hair, skin, and blood samples that a victim clawed from a rapist have been analyzed by police technicians and sometimes have aided identification. A button torn from clothing may match up with buttons still on the shirt or coat of a suspect caught nearby.

Occasionally a woman who has been forced to the rapist's car or residence manages to tear off one of her earrings, her buttons, or some hair, and hide it under a mattress, cushion, or car seat. If the police can subsequently find the hidden item, the case against the rapist will be stronger.

If you are attacked in your own home, examine the scene as soon as you are able to. Surprisingly, a rapist often leaves a key ring, comb, billfold, piece of jewelry, or hair specimen at the place where the struggle occurred.

Some women have helped convict a rapist by remembering specific physical details about him. Any scars, even small ones, may help to identify. Moles, birthmarks, tattoos, color of hair and eyes, length and waviness of hair, shape of face, missing or stained teeth, length of fingernails, height, weight, general build, suntan, the use of glasses or a disguise can all help law enforcement agents to catch and convict a rapist.

Protecting Evidence

Most people are not too sure what information is valuable to the police or the prosecutor. Therefore, it is best to leave the scene of the attack exactly as it was at the time of the assault. Make sure that friends, neighbors, or relations who come to your assistance do not rearrange furniture, pick up or touch anything unnecessarily. All your clothing, and especially your underclothing, should be saved for evidence.

The standard police procedure is to have a doctor give the victim a pelvic examination. The doctor who gives the exam will be looking for lacerations and for the presence of sperm. The doctor will ask you questions. You have the right to have a woman police officer present, and almost every police department will let you have a friend with you.

If you are the victim in a case of this kind, you will undoubtedly be questioned by the investigating police detective. This may be the second time you are questioned by the police about the facts, as another police officer is most likely to have taken the original complaint. The detective investigating the case may ask you to give a signed statement. This is in line with usual procedures. However, if you wish to have a policewoman present, you should insist on it at the outset of the interview.

You are never under a legal obligation to take a polygraph test (lie detector), although at times the police may request that this be done. If there is little or no outside evidence to corroborate your description of the attack, it might be wise to ask for a polygraph examination. In this situation, you want the police, doctors, and prosecutors to have every possible assurance that you are completely in the right.

Prosecution Differences

Experienced prosecutors know that it is often difficult to convict a rapist. The case may be relatively straightforward when a victim is attacked by a complete stranger, and police records in larger cities indicate that well over half of all rape complaints involve such victims. But it is usually considerably more difficult to get a conviction if the woman was raped by someone she accepted a date with, someone she allowed in her apartment, or someone she had a drink with at a bar.

In this kind of situation, the defense attorney will usually attempt to persuade the jury that the woman changed her mind after initial resistance. Since the law says that no rape has occurred if the woman consents in the end, even if some initial force is used, the defense will argue that this is what happened.

Sometimes the defense will try to create the impression that the victim "slept around" quite a bit, as if this justifies rape. The defense then suggests that the rapist is just one more man in the woman's life. The next step is for the defense to seek to raise the question, "Why should this woman single out this particular man to bring charges against?"

For many years, some defense attorneys have used a notorious old quotation that was supposedly permitted in English courts. As usually quoted, this statement is: "Rape is an accusation easily to be made and hard to be proved."[3] In fact, this idea is not a principle of rape law, and in several states in the United States, repeating this quotation to the jury has been banned.

Victim Harassment

The defendant, of course, must always be given a fair trial. This is a basic principle in any criminal prosecution when an individual's freedom is at stake. But at the same time, a rape prosecution should never be allowed to turn into an inquisition or a persecution of the victim. There are times when a defense attorney, unless stopped by the judge, will base the defense on harassment of the victim rather than on facts. All too often in the past, this kind of tactic has subjected the victim to such abuse that she has been flustered or distraught, becoming unable to remember the facts. Sometimes she has simply refused to go on with testimony that would nail down the case.

Observers of the judicial scene are in general agreement that the courts today are less inclined to let the defense go beyond reasonable limits. In one incident that received wide publicity in recent years, a state judge was recalled from office after exhibiting complete disregard for the feelings of a rape victim. Progress has also resulted from campaigns conducted by nationwide women's groups, which publicize the fact that the rights of the rape victim warrant special consideration.

Over the years, judges have traditionally taken the attitude that a single woman was either a virgin or completely promiscuous. Until recent times, the courts have generally reasoned that a woman's prior sexual history has a bearing on whether she gave her consent in a

[3]Usually attributed to Lord Matthew Hale (1609–1676), an English judge. This statement is sometimes called "Lord Hale's Instructions."

particular instance. In recent years, however, several states have passed laws that specifically prevent questions during the trial about the victim's prior sex life, except questions about the victim's possible prior relationship with the accused. Under California law, for example, the defense attorney must make a motion offering to present evidence of the victim's prior unchastity, and the judge conducts a hearing concerning this prospective evidence out of the presence of the jury. Unless the defense attorney can convince the judge that there is real merit to the claim of the victim's prior unchastity during this hearing, the matter cannot be heard or considered by the jury (California Penal Code, Sec. 261).

The New York courts hold that evidence concerning the victim's sexual conduct in a rape prosecution is not admissible unless (among other exceptions) it proves: (1) specific instances of the victim's prior sexual conduct with the accused, or (2) that the victim has been convicted of prostitution (New York Criminal Procedure Law, Sec. 60.42). Additional changes in state laws will undoubtedly be made in the future to prevent unwarranted humiliation of the victim of this crime.

Police Sensitivity

In recent years, an increasing number of police departments have begun "sensitivity training" sessions, aimed at making rank-and-file police officers more sympathetic to and understanding of the rape victim. Many police agencies have also set up special rape investigation units that are able to function with more understanding and efficiency in handling witnesses and problems of the prosecution. Additional improvements in this area should continue.

New Penalties for Rape

Some criminologists feel that penalties for rape in a few states may be extreme. They argue, for example, that the mandatory life sentence in some jurisdictions may constitute excessive punishment in certain cases. Because of such a severe mandatory sentence, a jury may simply refuse to find a rapist guilty, when the jury would likely find the man guilty if a shorter sentence could be considered. If the law provided for a sentence of from two to 10 years, for example, a higher percentage of convictions could probably be obtained. Changes in penalties to be imposed in some states may be worth consideration.

Crisis Centers

Women's organizations throughout the United States are setting up increasing numbers of crisis centers to aid the rape victim. Although much of this help is outside the scope of the legal process, these centers can be an important source of both emotional and legal help to rape victims. Besides working for legal reforms, these crisis centers usually maintain a telephone hotline for emergency advice. They give psychological support and offer immediate advice on hospital services, medical assistance, legal procedures, and general counseling. These centers also give self-defense training and rape prevention seminars and courses, as well as community educational services.

chapter 8

Living Together

common problems

POSSIBLE INDUCEMENTS FOR COHABITATION

Since the 1960s, there has been a substantial increase in the number of men and women living together outside of marriage, especially in larger cities. Some observers point out that most of these arrangements arise from three types of situations:

1. Individuals in a trial marriage arrangement.
2. Persons who would suffer financial loss through marriage, owing to reduced social security, pensions, or income; others may live together to reduce household expenses.
3. Individuals who prefer this arrangement to the long-term, permanent legal commitment of marriage.

THE ARRANGEMENT LEGAL OR ILLEGAL?

As live-in relationships have increased, so has public acceptance of the arrangement. But whether or not society approves, no one should become involved in a relationship of this kind without understanding some of the legal consequences that may arise from it.

In the first place, a live-in relationship is still simply illegal in a great many areas. Most states have laws making it a crime for a man and woman to be parties to illicit intercourse if either is married to a third person. This is the so-called crime of *adultery*, which was placed on the law books in most states many years ago and is still the law in most jurisdictions. Typical is the old statute, California Penal Code, Sec. 269a and 269b (Codified 1905): Every person who lives in a state of cohabitation and adultery is guilty of a misdemeanor and punishable by a fine not exceeding one thousand dollars, or by imprisonment in the county jail not exceeding one year, or both.

Roughly one-third of the states have another law prohibiting any sexual act between unmarried people of the opposite sex. This is a crime usually called *fornication*. Some states have statutes prohibiting *illicit cohabitation*, which the law usually describes as living together in a relation of either adultery or fornication.

Under Title 19 U.S. Code, Sec. 2421, it is a federal crime to transport a woman across a state line for sexual purposes. This law is sometimes known as the White Slave Traffic Act or the Mann Act (after Congressman Mann, the author of the law). The law was originally aimed at preventing pimps from transporting prostitutes across state lines. But over the years, the federal courts have not limited the application of this law to people intent on sexual activity for pay, or to the transportation of prostitutes alone. The courts have upheld convictions in which a man transported a woman whom he had lived with from one state to another.[1]

All this does not mean that unmarried couples who live together are apt to end up in jail. Neither the state nor the federal laws already mentioned are likely to be used to prosecute people in an ordinary

[1]Caminetti v. U.S., 242 U.S. 470; U.S. v. Caesar, 369 F. Supp. 328; Gebardi v. United States, 287 U.S. 112; Langford v. United States, 178 F. 2d 48.

live-in arrangement. But the fact that the relationship may be illegal can lead to a great many complications. For example, lawyers suggest that it is not advisable for a divorced parent with child custody to become involved in a live-in arrangement. The child's other parent may be able to use the fact of the live-in relationship as the basis for a successful custody suit.

COMMON LEGAL PROBLEMS

When a woman and a man decide they want to live together, there are a number of potential legal problems that should be avoided, or at least made note of. If you fall behind in your rent or lease payments, or merely break up the living arrangement, the landlord can sue both people who rented the property or whose signatures are on the lease.

If you acquire property—a stereo, furniture, and other household items, there may be problems. Lawyers usually advise people in an arrangement of this kind to make purchases individually. If you follow this procedure, the person paying for the items is the legal owner. If it is necessary for the couple to pool resources in order to make purchases, a serious dispute about ownership may arise if the relationship is terminated. On the whole, it may be best for live-in partners to have a written contract regarding property ownership such as the one on p. 81.

Sometimes insurance companies decline to issue fire insurance policies on furnishings and household goods owned in a nonmarital arrangement. Fire and burglary insurance companies state that claim losses are abnormally high when the insured persons live together without marriage; however, these companies do not explain the basis for this statement. Automobile insurance companies may refuse to grant coverage on the automobile of an unmarried couple.

If one of you requires emergency medical treatment or hospitalization, doctors and hospitals will frequently not accept an unmarried partner's written permission to treat.

CHILDREN BORN TO UNMARRIED PARENTS

Our social system still places a heavy penalty on a child born of unmarried parents—a penalty that the child in no way deserves. Regardless of changes in attitudes that have been made in recent years, an infant born out of wedlock will always bear a certain stigma with some individuals.

SAMPLE PROPERTY OWNERSHIP AGREEMENT

It is understood and agreed by ______________________________ and ______________________________ that we will share equally in the ownership of any property, furniture, or household furnishings acquired while living together.

Clothing and personal items will belong to the individual using such items.

The income and non-personal items acquired by either shall be shared equally, whether real estate or personal property. If we should separate, all accumulated property shall be divided equally.

In case of an inheritance by either of us, this inheritance shall remain the separate property of the one receiving it. If we should separate, neither of us thereafter has any claim to property or money.

______________________________ ______________________________

dated______________________________ dated______________________________

A child born outside of marriage has the same right to support that other children have. But the operation of legal machinery is often unable to compel a father to pay if there is no marriage record. First, paternity must be established, and the mother may have difficulty in legally establishing who the father is. This proof would not be needed if the child was born in a marital relationship. An infant born under these circumstances may be subjected to undeserved embarrassment from the time a birth certificate is needed for admission to primary school.

When a child is born outside of marriage, lawyers frequently advise the parents to go through a wedding ceremony immediately. This can be wise, even if the parents file for divorce immediately afterward. If the parents do marry, the courts usually treat the infant as always having been legitimate.

A child born outside marriage may have problems in inheriting property when one of the parents dies, although the property is rightfully due to the child. This is a complicated legal subject beyond the scope of this book. And, for example, if the father should be killed accidentally, the mother may have difficulty establishing social security benefits for herself and her child. In summary, being born outside of marriage places some considerable financial risks on the child. (For more information on the legal standing of children born outside of marriage, see Chapter 18.)

DIVIDING PROPERTY WHEN A LIVE-IN RELATIONSHIP TERMINATES

An unmarried couple can have serious problems when they divide the property they have accumulated. For a great many years, the basic approach of English and American courts was that a woman could not expect to claim any property or money from her live-in partner unless she eventually married him. A generation or two ago, the courts in this country were still uniformly quite severe in their attitudes toward any woman claiming property in a live-in relationship. One old judge was assigned to hand down a property decision, based on an unmarried woman's claim that she was entitled to half of the property acquired in the years that she lived with a man. In his written decision, this New York State Appellate judge said, "It is difficult to imagine a more audacious challenge to a court of justice . . . than that which appears in this complaint by this woman" (*Vincent* v. *Moriarty*, 52 N.Y S. 520). Needless to say, she did not get the property.

In most instances, the court's reasoning in these cases was based on their interpretation of contract law. It has always been a fundamental principle of contract law that a contract would not be enforced, or recognized by the courts, if part of the consideration (part of the bargain on either side) called for the performance of some illegal act. In applying this principle, the courts said that an arrangement to live together was a violation of state laws prohibiting adultery and/or fornication. Therefore, part of the agreement to live together was unlawful, and the courts would not enforce any contract or agreement based on that relationship.

In summarizing these old attitudes of a generation or two ago, one court noted that: "(nonmarital partners) cannot lawfully contract to pay for the performance of sexual services, for such a contract is, in essence, an agreement for prostitution, and unlawful for that reason." Another court said: ". . . a court will not enforce a contract for the pooling of property and earnings if it is explicitly and inseparably based upon services as a paramour" (*Shaw* v. *Shaw*, 227 Cal. App. 2d 159; *Hill* v. *Estate of Westbrook*, 247 P. 2d 19; *Updeck* v. *Samuel*, 266 P. 2d 822). And still another court summarized: "Historically, courts have been reluctant to grant relief of any kind to a party who was involved in what was termed a 'meretricious' (live-in partnership) relationship. Courts took the position that the parties had entered into a relationship outside the bounds of law, and the courts would not allow themselves to be used to solve the property disputes evolving from that relationship. Generally, the parties were left as they were when they came to court, with ownership resting in whoever happened to have title or possession at the time." But by 1973, a number of courts were holding that the old approach was no longer valid. For example, in 1973 a Michigan court held that although cohabitation is a crime in that state, there was nothing illegal about a contract merely because the people making the agreement were living together. In the words of the court:

> Where a meretricious relationship (live-in arrangement) has already been entered upon, to penalize one of the parties by striking down their otherwise lawful promises, will not undo the relationship, nor is it likely to discourage others from entering upon such relationships (*Tyranski* v. *Piggins*, 205 N.W. 2d 595).

In the much publicized case of *Marvin* v. *Marvin*, 557 P. 2d 106 (1976), the Supreme Court of California seemed to be writing new law. The case involved a lawsuit by Michelle Triola Marvin against a well-known movie actor, Lee Marvin. After they had lived together for approximately six years, they split up, and the plaintiff, Michelle Marvin, went to court, claiming that she and Lee Marvin had made an oral contract at the time they started living together. Michelle stated that, in this contract, she agreed to give up her career and devote her full time to Lee as homemaker, companion, cook, and housekeeper. In return, she claimed that Lee promised to provide for all her financial needs for the rest of her life.

The relationship between Michelle and Lee ended in 1970. Michelle moved out, but Lee continued to pay her support money of $800 a month for over a year. When Lee cut off these payments, Michelle filed suit, claiming that she was entitled to half of the millions Lee had made in movie rights. Michelle's attorney based this suit on Michelle's claim that she was entitled to the money under the terms of the original oral contract.

When the matter went before the trial court, Lee Marvin denied that he had made an oral contract with Michelle. And some of the evidence suggested that the career Michelle had allegedly given up had offered considerably less promise of financial reward than Lee Marvin's career did.

Some of the top lawyers in the country are not quite sure what the California Supreme Court was saying in *Marvin* v. *Marvin*. But it appears that the court intended to state the following:

1. Unmarried couples have the right to make express oral contracts concerning how they want their property handled, in the event the relationship ends.

2. Unmarried couples may have formed a contract that may be inferred from all the circumstances of the living arrangement. This means that, even if a written or spoken contract could not be found, the trial judge would be entitled to presume such a contract was intended, considering all the facts and inferences from their treatment of each other and the facts surrounding their life.

3. Unmarried couples owe something to each other in a monetary way, as an outgrowth of their living arrangement. This would be true

even though an express contract could not be found from the facts, and even if an implied understanding or contract could not be spelled out or inferred from the life circumstances of the parties.

The court indicated that a recovery of some sort would be due to the live-in mate, based on "some kind of judgment of merit." In passing, the court mentioned the legal theories of "quantum meruit" and a "constructive trust" or "resulting trust." All of these are novel theories that have never had legal application in a situation of this kind.

The phrase *quantum meruit* is an old Latin legal expression that is usually translated to mean "as much as is merited by the circumstances." A *constructive trust,* or *resulting trust,* is a trust fund recognized, implied, or raised up by the courts from all the circumstances of a transaction. It is a way of making a money award to someone when there is no real justification under contract or tort law, but when justice demands the award.

The practical information we should draw from the court's tortured reasoning in the *Marvin* case is that people who live together should write out a simple contract stating who is to own specific property if they break up. This kind of contract could be written in two or three sentences; so long as the meaning is clear, no specific wording is needed. It should be signed and dated by both people involved. A typical contract that would avoid the controversy of *Marvin* v. *Marvin* appears on p. 81.

Future Application of the Marvin Decision

The legal approach followed in *Marvin* v. *Marvin* was extended somewhat by the Oregon Supreme Court in *Beal* v. *Beal* and by the Minnesota Supreme Court in *Carlson* v. *Olson*, 256 N.W. 2. In the Carlson opinion the court pointed out:

> . . . This appeal raises the issue of the assertion of property rights based on nonmarital domestic relations entered into . . . Oral Olson . . . and Laura Carlson began to live together . . . at the time she was 22 and he was 31. They lived together for 21 years, raised a son to majority, and acquired a modest home and some property. They did not, however, ever legally marry, although they did hold themselves out to neighbors, friends, relatives, and the public as man and wife. During the relationship she did not work outside the home. In 1974 differences arose

> between the parties. She no longer wanted to reside with him and desired a share of the property. To accomplish this, she brought an action to partition [legally divide] their real and personal property. . . During their cohabitation he furnished all the actual monies for the acquisition and improvement of the real estate, the personal property located thereon, and the personal effects of the parties, with the exception of $1,000 supplied by her mother...

After going into the facts, the Supreme Court of Minnesota held that Laura Carlson was entitled to half of all the couple's accumulated property. The court said this division was based on the theory that the parties had an agreement to share the accumulations, and that the contributions of each was an irrevocable gift to the other of one-half of the assets in both real estate and of the household and other personal properties as well.

Some legal authorities predict that the basic ideas of the *Marvin* and *Carlson* cases will be widely adopted as law in other states. Other lawyers, however, are not so sure. For other states to hold that a live-in arrangement confers an automatic right to compensation for a nonworking partner would mean overturning decisions that have consistently been to the contrary for many years. Attorneys point out that a switch to the Marvin holding would disturb property rights that people have considered settled for years. People make decisions that affect their money and property, based on what they understand the law to be. Rightly or wrongly, in the past men have sometimes deliberately chosen a live-in arrangement rather than a marriage because they did not wish to settle a substantial interest in their money or property on the woman. The court in the *Marvin* case seemed to be saying that it would award the woman some of the man's property, even though he deliberately chose this arrangement knowing that she could not expect a wife's rights.

Some critics of the *Marvin* v. *Marvin* decision state that in many areas of this country the general public is simply not ready for the courts to give financial awards to individuals trying to benefit from what is still widely regarded as a crime (fornication or adultery). Others have pointed out that the California court seemed to be, in effect, nullifying the meaning of the Statute of Frauds. This statute, as followed in most states, provides that an unwritten contract is unenforceable if the value of the contract is in excess of $500.

Still other lawyers point out that the *Marvin* decision is a prime example of "judge-made law" through a court decision. They argue that if new rights are in need of legal recognition, it is up to the legislature to provide them. Law making is not within the province of the courts.

COMMON LAW MARRIAGE

Marriages in early England were performed exclusively by church officials. By the seventeenth century, the time of Oliver Cromwell and John Milton, many English political leaders said that the Catholic Church was meddling, attempting to run all the affairs of government and dictate to the English throne. In 1653 the British Parliament passed the "Civil Marriage Ordinance Act," a law that required all English marriages to be performed by a justice of the peace. When the Pilgrims and other settlers brought English law to the American colonies, a clergyman could not legally celebrate a marriage. This prohibition continued for a number of years. But after a time, the colonial governments in New England began to recognize a marriage as legal if it was performed either by a recognized clergyman or by a government official designated for that function. This, of course, is the system that still prevails throughout the United States today.

So-called common law marriages were recognized in England when the colonists came to this country. Consequently, the idea also gained legal recognition on the America frontier. Often, neither clergy nor justices of the peace were available. Besides, a couple that wanted to get married might be hundreds of miles from the nearest place where a marriage license could be obtained.

As the frontier developed, approximately half of the states in the United States came to regard common law marriages as valid. The states that did were generally in the newly developing areas of the West. In recent years, however, some jurisdictions have outlawed common law marriages. Today, they are still recognized in about one-third of the states.

The courts have always said that common law marriages would be recognized only under specific conditions. Judges have always agreed that merely living together in a sexual arrangement is never sufficient to prove a common law marriage. The following requirements have been spelled out by court decisions:

1. The couple must live together in a marital state (*Maher* v. *Maher*, 14 N.Y.S. 2d 559).
2. The couple must not only admit that their intentions were matrimonial, (*De Shazo* v. *Christian*, 191 So. 2d 495; *In re Jacobsen's estate*, 39A. 2d 704), but must take action to create public recognition that their acts and intentions were matrimonial (*Crocket* v. *Consolidated Paper Co.*, 274 N.W. 253, holding that common law marriage requires publicity of the fact).
3. They must assume matrimonial responsibilities and obligations, not merely live together (*State ex. rel. Smith* v. *Superior Court of King County*, 161 P. 2d 188).

Some courts have said that the parties claiming a common law marriage must live in the same residence. But the court decisions have consistently held that merely living together in a "meretricious relationship" is never a sufficient basis for a common law marriage (*Pickett* v. *Pickett*, 161 P. 2d 520; the Linseed King, D.C.N.Y., 48 F. 2d 311, 42 F. 2d 129, 285 U.S. 52). However, cohabitation is an element of common law marriage. (Legally, a meretricious relationship means a merely sexual arrangement.) And the decisions have said that merely having a reputation throughout the community of being married is not enough—some positive action to assert the marriage claim must be made by the couple themselves. A mere undercurrent of rumor is not enough (*In re Price's estate*, 176 So. 492). Simply introducing each other as man and wife is not sufficient, when an issue is made of the relationship (*City of New York* v. *Landau*, 221 N.Y.S. 189; *Honore* v. *Jones*, 156 So. 191).

In short, the courts have required that a common law marriage must be inferred from the facts in each case, and the intent to be treated as though married must be clear and determinable from the couple's continued course of conduct. Generally, no limit of time for the continuance of this relationship has been imposed by the courts, so long as the parties' intent has been clear to all the world.

The fact that a man and woman at first lived together without intending to marry does not mean that they could not subsequently contract a common law marriage. Whether the parties later intended such a change would have to be determined from all the available facts (*U.S. Fidelity and Guaranty Company* v. *Henderson*, 53 S.W.

2d 811). And resuming sexual relations after a couple has been divorced does not, standing alone, constitute a common law marriage (*Reppert* v. *Reppert*, 241 NW 487).

Lawyers usually say that there are no absolutely certain ways for the parties to a common law marriage to prove that they had the required intent to form such a union. Such an intention can almost always be proven, however, in those states where common law marriages are recognized, by some or all of the following:

- Using the same last name.
- Publicly advising everyone that they are married.
- Living in the same residence.
- Maintaining a joint bank account.
- Paying tax returns together.
- Listing the other as beneficiary, wife, husband, or next of kin on insurance policies, annuities, and the like.
- Having a joint car registration.
- Listing their names as "Mr. and Mrs." on the mail box.
- Attending functions such as PTA meetings as "parents" of a child.

Once the common law requirements for marriage have been met, the marriage is in existence. It can legally be ended only by divorce, legal separation, or other procedures followed by state law.

Common Law Marriage Recognized As Valid By Other States

Article IV, Section 1 of the United States Constitution states that "Full faith and credit shall be given in each state to the public acts, records, and judicial proceedings of every other state." Accordingly, any state that does not provide for common law marriage within its own laws will recognize such a marriage if it was properly formed in a state that does permit this kind of marriage. For example, a couple lived together in Alabama, where their relationship was regarded as a common law marriage. On moving to Illinois, where common law marriages are not permitted, the courts would still regard the couple as legally married. The law that controls is the law of the state from which the couple came.

When a man and woman have formed a valid common law marriage and they move to a state where such a union is not recognized, it may, however, be legally advisable to go through a formal marriage ceremony in the new state. Such a precaution may avoid a great many possible legal complications in the future—if children are born, if the couple purchases property, if one inherits at the time of the other's death, and so on.

Problems with Common Law Marriages

Legal scholars and courts have never been very sympathetic toward common law unions. As one judge said: "Nothing muddies the legal waters as much as a claim of a common law marriage." The courts point out that if a couple really wants to be married, they should encounter no problem in finding a justice of the peace to perform a ceremony.

Unless the alleged marriage has become the subject of a lawsuit that resulted in a court adjudication, there will be no record that a common law marriage took place. With no record, it may later be very difficult to prove that such a marriage was ever formed, if proof is needed. For example, a couple lived together for several years. The man and the woman both died, leaving no wills. Since they had no children, the woman's sister claimed to be the only heir for both the man and the woman. The sister went into court and maintained that a common law marriage existed and that on the husband's death, the wife inherited the man's property. As the woman's heir, the sister claimed that all the property of both the man and the woman passed to her. All of the sister's claims may well have been true. But after the couple is dead, who is to say that they intended to form a common law marriage?

All too often, the courts know that a couple may live together with no intent of ever marrying. Then, if the man should die, the woman may realize for the first time that she needs to prove a common law marriage in order to inherit his property, to collect death benefits under workman's compensation laws, or to qualify as a beneficiary under a social security pension. After the death of one of the parties, the truth may be unclear.

Then too, the courts are regularly faced with a variety of situations in which a child born outside of marriage could be legitimized by a subsequent court judgment that a common law marriage had taken place. In such cases, the courts almost invariably strive to reach a judgment holding that there was a common law marriage. But this cannot always be done without straining the facts. In some cases, the court cannot hold that a common law marriage was formed without working a serious injustice on the rights of others who may be involved in a legal controversy.

Accordingly, a number of states have repealed laws that recognized common law marriage. They have done so because, as one judge put it: "The common law marriage idea has done nothing but cause endless controversy when marital records can quickly establish legal rights." It is also worth noting that the *Marvin* case might well have been decided on the assumption that a common law marriage had been formed, but common law marriage has not been recognized in California for a number of years.

chapter 9

The Marital Breakup

separation, annulment, divorce

Once a marriage has taken place, the union can be dissolved only by the death of one of the partners or by divorce, annulment, or separation. (Separation in itself does not dissolve a legal marriage, but it is often the first step in the eventual breakup.) All too often a marital breakup is the end of a dream begun as a joyful partnership. In the dissolution process, both husband and wife tend to look at the past through different windows. At best, the affair is a public confession of failure in a private, highly personal relationship. But to compel people to continue to live together in conflict may be a doubtful strategy for society and of no benefit to the people involved.

Emotions sometimes run very high when a marriage begins to break apart. The stakes involved for both man and woman may be particularly important. Children are sometimes reduced to having one effective parent, and they may be torn between the individual parents' demands for custody. Financial security that has been planned for years may be put in jeopardy. Divorces almost invariably lead to bitterness, a stifling of love, and a loss of community prestige.

In a great many instances, the woman may have a harder time in walking away from the marriage relationship than the man. Frequently, this is because the husband may continue in a somewhat comparable life-style, while the woman may not be able to do so. During marriage the male is usually in charge of most of the couple's financial resources. But in case of divorce or separation, the woman may find that she has little in the way of money control or financial clout. Too often she feels that she has spent a number of important years of her life helping her husband to build everything he has—and now she is to be left with nothing.

Nevertheless, wives continue to insist on divorces. About three-fourths of current divorces are asked for by women, and granted to women.

Some individuals argue that the institution of marriage may actually be breaking down. They point to the fact that approximately one-third of all marriages in the United States will eventually end in divorce. Generally, the larger the city, the higher the divorce rate. Statistics maintained in some areas reflect that there are more divorces than marriages in certain years. The increase in divorce is explained by some as evidence that people today are less willing to tolerate unhappiness in marriage than were prior generations. Regardless of the reasons and motivations for marital breakups, a good number of people regard divorce as a necessary escape route.

DISSOLVING MARRIAGE IN ENGLISH LAW

Divorce law in the United States, like almost all of our legal system, is based on the divorce law of England. Divorce, as we know it, was not permitted by the early English courts. The only way of terminating a marriage was annulment—in effect, declaring that the marriage never took place. Annulment was granted by high Church authorities, but only sparingly.

One of the most celebrated annulments in history involved Henry VIII (1491–1547), the strong-willed king of the then Catholic country of England. Henry began to tire of his aging, foreign-born wife, Catherine (the marriage had taken place at least in part to cement political ties with Spain). He began to express doubts about the "propriety" of his marriage; Catherine had been his deceased brother's wife. More pertinent, however, were two other facts: Henry was growing increasingly obsessed with the fact that he had no son as heir to the throne (at that time, it was not at all certain that a woman would be legally able to inherit the English crown); and the king wished to marry Anne Boleyn, one of his wife's ladies-in-waiting.

Henry applied to the Pope in Rome for a divorce or annulment, but he was refused. Because of Church doctrine, the Pope did not favor any kind of legal termination of marriage. Also, the Pope did not believe it politic to side against Catherine, daughter of the then-powerful king of Spain.

Stubborn and impetuous, Henry turned to Thomas Cranmer, official of the Catholic Church in England. Perhaps as much politician as churchman, Cranmer declared Henry's marriage to Catherine null and void. The Pope bitterly protested that one of his underlings could not do what he himself would not. To give Cranmer's decision more backing, Henry VIII had the English Parliament vote him an annulment from Catherine.

Henry went on to set up the Church of England as a separate church, with himself as the head. And from about that time on, the English courts recognized the validity of two kinds of legal separation: (1) *divorce a mensa et thoro*, sometimes called "a divorce from table and bed," in substance, a kind of legal separation that stopped short of actual divorce; and (2) *divorce a vinculo matrimoni*, a complete separation from all the bonds of marriage. The English courts put some very restrictive requirements on both of these kinds of separation. Those requirements need not concern us here, except as they still have an influence on modern legal requirements. These two types of separation continued to be the only ones recognized by the English or American courts for hundreds of years. Today, legal systems in the United States recognize three different ways of terminating the marriage arrangement: separation, annulment, and divorce. All three have different legal requirements and legal implications, and are discussed in the rest of this chapter.

SEPARATION

A separation may be the first step in a dissolution, but it does not end a marriage. In a typical situation of this kind, a couple may voluntarily sign a written legal contract to maintain separate living quarters, to care for and educate their children, and to agree to divide property. This stops the couple's right to sexual relations, but it does not alter other basic marital rights or legal obligations. And the couple can sign another agreement, repudiating all that was agreed to in the first contract.

However, so long as an agreement of this kind is outstanding, the spouses can no longer live in the same living quarters or cohabit at any place. In the words of the old English courts, the spouses are "separated from table and board." The husband and wife are required to live apart, both in a sexual sense and in their living arrangements. Within this arrangement, the couple continues to be married. Should one of the spouses violate the terms of the contract, the other spouse may sue for money damages for breach of contract.

In about three-fourths of the states, there are laws that provide for separation under orders of a court. This kind of separation is begun as a lawsuit by one spouse. This is sometimes called a *formal separation*. There is no mutual agreement or contract between the spouses here. As an outgrowth of the separation lawsuit filed by one spouse, the terms of the separation agreement are spelled out by the judge hearing the case. If either side thereafter commits acts contrary to the judge's decree, the other spouse can apply to the judge to have the court orders complied with. This, of course, will be done almost automatically by the judge.

Under a court-ordered separation decree, the couple may continue to live apart indefinitely. But at times a separation decree is a halfway measure leading to divorce.

In those states that do not have laws providing for court-ordered separation decrees, the courts will still uphold a couple's contract for a separation agreement, if the agreement is properly drawn. But the basic difference is that in those states without laws for judicial separation, the basic agreement is upheld as a contract right and not as a court order. It is also to be noted that a court separation agreement prior to a divorce decree may settle the questions of alimony, child support, or division of property.

Desertion

A desertion of a wife or husband by the other mate is a form of separation. In legal or social work circles, this is sometimes termed "a poor man's divorce." Neither spouse has the right to marry following a desertion without first obtaining a divorce or annulment. The husband's usual legal obligation to support a deserted wife and children continues indefinitely, regardless of where the husband goes. And whenever the missing spouse returns, both parties still have the right to resume their marital relations, unless a divorce or legal separation has intervened.

In many states, a deserted wife may sue for separate maintenance and support money as soon as it is apparent that she has been deserted. She may also be awarded control of the family dwelling or home and contents by the courts, as well as custody of the children. To do this, however, the wife ordinarily needs help from an attorney. If the wife does sue for separate maintenance and support money, the missing husband cannot return and resume the marital relationship unless the wife consents to take him back.

Desertion is grounds for divorce in most states. And if a wife has begun a legal separation action in the courts, she is generally permitted to claim both alimony and attorney's fees for her lawyer if the matter proceeds on through a divorce action.

It is almost always desirable to have a separation agreement (contract) drawn by an attorney. Some lawyers specializing in divorce and separation matters point out that a separation action (lawsuit) in itself frequently accomplishes little from a legal standpoint and that it is better for the couple to work out their differences as soon as possible or to continue on to obtain a divorce.

ANNULMENT

An annulment is the only legal technique recognized by the Roman Catholic Church for ending a marriage. Annulment laws vary greatly from state to state. In some localities that have a large percentage of residents of the Catholic faith, some annulment laws have many features of divorce laws in other states.

We noted earlier that an annulment is an adjudication by a court that a marriage never happened in the first place. A divorce presupposes a valid marriage. An annulment is a legal holding that the ceremony was somehow invalid at the time it was held. An annulment wipes out the entire past of the marriage arrangement, and in many states it places the parties back in the legal status at the time the marriage ceremony took place.

Frequently, an annulment is permitted by the laws only if one party can convince the court that the union was entered into through a fraud committed by the other party. For example, a woman could expect to obtain an annulment from a man she married if it turned out that he had concealed the fact that he was already married. Similarly, an annulment would probably be granted to an unknowing wife who subsequently learned her husband had covered up a life of prior crime. But an annulment would not likely be granted by the courts if the man said he was 32 years old when he was already 35. Some courts would, however, permit an annulment if the man was actually penniless, but had represented himself to be the owner of a business and the majority stockholder in a neighborhood bank. And as a general rule, courts may allow an annulment if one spouse learns that the other spouse's claim of prior chastity was false.

As we noted, there are wide differences from state to state in annulment laws. Frequently, the courts are reluctant to grant an annulment. These courts operate on the idea that an action of this kind must be based on fraud in the inducement of the marital agreement. Judges often refuse an annulment if there is no evidence of substantial fraud, or if the claimed basis was simply that one of the partners felt cheated in their marital expectations. For an annulment, the courts sometimes say that the fraud must be clear, it must be substantial in nature, and that it must go to the very heart of the marital agreement.

Most courts in all states are also reluctant to decree an annulment if the marriage has existed for some time and if children have been born to the union. Judges will generally refuse an annulment if the complaining spouse has continued to live in a married state with the offending spouse for any considerable time after learning of the supposed fraud. In short, the courts seldom grant an annulment if the complaining party has condoned or in any way accepted the action of the offending spouse.

There is also considerable variance in the way courts treat the legal and financial responsibilities of a couple in granting an annulment. Property settlements approved by the courts are sometimes difficult to work out if the couple has been married more than a short time. In any event, a lawyer's help is needed in handling an annulment. A good number of courts say that when an annulment is decreed, the parties are put back in exactly the same financial and legal status they enjoyed at the time of the marriage. This is not always true, however, especially if there are offspring as a result of the union.

Rules of the Roman Catholic Church permit a church-sanctified union to be annulled, but these rules never allow recognition of divorce. To accommodate these church requirements, a number of states have annulment laws that resemble divorce laws in other states. States with liberal annulment statutes specify a number of conditions that will be recognized by the courts as fraud of the kind to obtain an annulment. These laws may specify some or all of the following situations:

1. Refusal of one spouse to have children.
2. Refusal to go through with church wedding as promised, after going through a civil ceremony.
3. Concealing the fact that the husband was not responsible for pregnancy.
4. Misrepresentation of prior chastity.
5. Concealment of a prior marriage or divorce.
6. Serious financial misrepresentations.
7. Concealment of venereal disease or serious illness.
8. Marriage motivated by use of the ceremony to become an American citizen.
9. Concealment of serious criminal record.
10. Any substantial fraud in inducing the other party to agree to marriage.

In general, states with very strict divorce laws are more liberal in their laws on annulment. Some states permit annulment for conditions or facts that occur after the marriage has taken place. Some additional facts that may qualify for annulment include:

1. Sterility of either husband or wife discovered after the ceremony, unless as a result of injury, accident, illness, or the like.
2. Refusal to make good on financial promises made to the other spouse before marriage.
3. Failure to keep a premarital agreement to change religion or to raise the offspring in a specified religious faith.
4. Insanity that developed after the marriage.
5. Incapability of one spouse to engage in sexual intercourse.

It should also be pointed out that a court handling a request for an annulment usually has wide latitude to grant or refuse it, even though the party requesting the action feels entitled to it as a matter of law. The court usually has an absolute right to do what is deemed best, considering the interests of society as a whole, as well as the individual lives of the spouses and children.

In most instances, but not always, the husband is required to support children born to a marriage that was subsequently annulled. Generally in cases of this kind, both the husband and wife are awarded separate property owned prior to marriage, and joint property is divided among them. Here again, the judge handling the matter usually has the right to exercise such discretion as is deemed fair.

Although it is not the general rule, there are a few states in which a child born to an annulled marriage is considered illegitimate and may not have the right to inherit property from the father. In addition, under the law in some states, the wife whose marriage is annulled may not be entitled to inherit property in her husband's estate, and she may not be granted alimony by the courts.

DIVORCE

Divorce is, of course, by far the most commonly used legal method for termination of marriage. Conditions under which people live in the large cities seem especially conducive to divorce, and it appears to be a way of life in the late twentieth century. Then too, attitudes change—many individuals no longer cling to the idea that marriage is an institution that should never be ended.

Legally, a divorce action is a civil court proceeding, or lawsuit, based on a claimed matrimonial wrong. The married parties are designated plaintiff and defendant, depending on which spouse claimed to have been wronged (*Gallemore* v. *Gallemore*, 114 So. 371).

There are wide differences in state laws concerning divorce, not only as to who is eligible to file for a divorce in terms of residence, but as to those grounds that will be recognized as sufficient legal cause. In some jurisdictions, it is very difficult to comply with legal requirements, while a divorce is comparatively easy to obtain in others.

States have authority to grant a divorce only to their own residents. In Nevada or Idaho, you may establish residence by living there for a period of no more than six weeks. At the other extreme, Massachusetts may require five years of residence to qualify. Apparently, at least some of these easy residence requirements were set up to lure individuals with money to the state. Those states with short residence requirements are sometimes known in legal circles as "divorce mill" states.

In most instances, a divorce action is usually started by the wife. But whichever spouse begins the action must first establish a legal residence where the divorce is to be obtained. When the papers are filed, the other spouse is notified. If the matter is not being contested, the lawyer for the defendant files a legal paper called a *notice of appearance,* and the proceeding goes on. The defending spouse may actually be thousands of miles away, but because of the filing of the notice of appearance, the court technically considers both parties as being before the court.

At this stage, if the action was begun by the wife, she may have her attorney ask the judge for a court order instructing the husband to pay temporary alimony for such period as it takes to settle the divorce matter. Legally, this kind of temporary alimony is called *alimony pendente lite.*

If the husband desires to contest the divorce, he may have his attorney file a legal paper called *an answer,* setting out grounds why a divorce should not be granted, or why alimony and property settlements should not be made. The filing of an answer may be followed by a conference between the judge and the two parties, in which the judge attempts to get both sides to agree to procedures or settlements that may reduce trial time.

In the great majority of divorce cases, the matter may never come to an actual trial. If there is a trial, either a jury or the judge may settle those facts that are in dispute. The case then proceeds to an adjudication of divorce by the judge, or is decided in favor of the defendant, depending on the evidence that came to light during the trial.

State Requirements

As noted, there are wide differences from state to state concerning the grounds that may be used by the courts to grant a divorce. For many years, courts in all states specified that these exacting requirements had to be proved beyond doubt. Until 1967, New York State would accept no legal basis for divorce except adultery. Many other states had very stringent requirements. Common to all these grounds was the basic idea that one spouse had done something wholly incompatible with the marriage contract or relationship—the idea that one spouse was at fault. Today, a considerable number of states still use this "fault concept," requiring proof of only a limited number of grounds. In general, the states that follow this "fault" idea limit divorce to behavior that involves adultery, conviction of a serious crime such as murder, robbery, or rape, continual drunkenness or drug addiction, nonsupport of a wife by a husband, or desertion for a substantial period of time. A few states also include insanity or "extreme cruelty" as additional grounds for divorce. Exactly what "extreme cruelty" consists of sometimes varies from state to state or from case to case. Some courts insist that extreme physical brutality must have occurred.

Grounds for Divorce Beyond "Fault"

Legislatures in some states became convinced that existing divorce laws were forcing people to live together in continuing misery. These states began to pass laws recognizing that both sides could be at fault, acknowledging that fault is immaterial in any event if the marriage has become completely unworkable.

Based on these liberalized laws, courts in some states began to grant divorces without proof that one spouse was at fault. Today, we say that a state has old-style, specific requirements for divorce, so-called no fault divorce laws, or a combination of both. In 1970, California passed legislation specifying two almost all-inclusive grounds for divorce: (1) irreconcilable differences or (2) incurable insanity. Lawyers sometimes say that *irreconcilable differences* are simply any conditions of incompatibility—an inability to get along. This, of course, is very easy to prove. It is simply a matter of having a wife or husband testify that the couple has been unable to get along.

Today, a considerable number of states have gone exclusively to no fault divorce requirements. Some states, however, still favor the old notion that fault must be proved in court. If you want a divorce, you must usually contact a local attorney to determine what grounds must exist in your state and whether it might be advantageous to go out of state for a divorce.

Lawyers feel that there is a definite trend for all states eventually to adopt no fault divorce laws. But this movement may be strongly resisted in some states. As a result, people who cannot afford to go to a "divorce mill" state may be forced to remain in a miserable marriage.

Legal systems in so-called fault divorce states usually impose needless problems on both the individuals seeking a divorce and on those officials who administer the legal system. To prove that fault existed, couples must frequently expose their marital secrets and problems to the public. And the fact of this exposure may greatly intensify the friction between the spouses, destroying whatever respect and trust still exists.

Then too, the parties involved, their lawyers, and the judge are all aware that a certain amount of rationalization enters the court in these fault cases. Charges of misconduct are sometimes made merely to satisfy the technicalities of the state divorce laws. Evidence may be "manufactured" to answer the legal requirements. And all of this creates an air of cynicism that the spouses may forever carry as an impression of the legal system.

Lawyers in some states point out that one of the most convincing arguments for no-fault divorce is that it eliminates the farce that may be necessary to establish grounds. Meanwhile, the judge courteously withholds probing into the evidence in order to get on with the case.

Defenses to Divorce

From a nationwide standpoint, only a small percentage of divorce suits are contested by the defendant. But if you are anticipating a divorce, you should realize that it may be contested if you live in a state where divorces are still based on fault. The legal defenses that are usually used are collusion or connivance, condonation, and recrimination.

Legally, *collusion* and *connivance* are defenses against divorce that mean the same thing. The courts have always spoken out in favor of the institution of marriage, and court decisions seem to lean toward preservation of it. In states where fault must be proved, it is not unusual for both husband and wife to connive or engage in collusion to set up the required grounds for the divorce suit. In a typical situation of this kind in the past, where adultery was the most commonly recognized grounds, the wife and a private investigator might stage a scene in which the husband was caught in a motel room with a prearranged lover. Actually, no adultery had taken place, but the private investigator could testify as to what had happened.

If an arrangement of this kind resulted from a scheme agreed to by both husband and wife, the courts would say that it was either connivance or collusion. If, during the divorce trial, the husband should reveal what actually happened, the court would refuse to grant a divorce.

Condonation is recognized as a defense to a divorce action in a number of states. This defense is perhaps the most effective and the most frequently used in those instances where one spouse opposes the divorce. Condonation is usually defined by the courts as a legal forgiveness by the injured spouses of the act or acts by the other mate that served as legal grounds for the divorce action. For example, a husband may give his wife legal grounds for a divorce through his acts of adultery. But on learning of these extracurricular acts, the wife may agree to continue to live with her husband as a wife. The wife's motives in staying with her husband are immaterial, so far as the law is concerned. By accepting him back as her husband and allowing him to share her bed again, the courts in some states say she has condoned his acts.

If the husband gives his wife no further grounds for divorce, he may claim the defense of condonation if the wife eventually decides to sue for divorce. But if the husband commits a new act of adultery, the courts say that the husband has renewed the wife's grounds for a divorce. Of course, if the wife continues to take the husband back every time, the defense of condonation would still be available to the husband.

Condonation is available to the defendant only in those states where fault must be proved. The legal philosophy of this defense is simply that one spouse may not in one instant ignore the offending spouse's behavior and in the next instant go into court seeking a divorce based on that wrongful behavior.

Recrimination is the legal idea that neither spouse should be granted a divorce if the other mate can also prove legally recognized grounds for a divorce action. For example, a husband regularly clubbed his wife with great brutality. Completely innocent of legal cause to this stage, the wife moved into the apartment of a newly acquired male friend, living in adultery with this man. This, it would appear, would give the husband grounds for divorce. But if the wife filed for a divorce based on great brutality, the husband could claim the defense of recrimination, pointing out that the wife was herself at fault in committing adultery. Recrimination is available as a defense to a divorce suit in those states where fault must be proven.

Recrimination, then, is an old legal principle that will not permit a divorce to either spouse, even though both clearly have legal grounds for such action. Some variations of the recrimination principle are allowed in 12 states where spousal fault must be proved to obtain a divorce. On principle, recrimination seems to be definitely unfair. Legal scholars believe that it may be phased out as an acceptable basis for a court defense in the forseeable future.

Divorce Decrees

In awarding a divorce, the judge may grant a *final decree* or an *interlocutory decree*, depending on state law. A final decree is effective immediately. An interlocutory decree becomes final within a specified period of time, usually within thirty, sixty, or ninety days. Within the period specified by an interlocutory decree, the individuals involved may not legally remarry, and they may be held in contempt for attempting to do so.

Do-It-Yourself Divorce

A great variety of do-it-yourself kits for obtaining a divorce have appeared in bookstores and magazines in recent years. Some include blank forms to be filled out and filed without a lawyer; others are limited to instructions and text materials. Undoubtedly some kits of this kind could have value. But the individual seeking a divorce without a lawyer is running the risk of forfeiting a number of future rights. These may include such benefits as pension rights or equities, company stock and social security benefits, and similar items. Then too, private individuals may not be able to work out legal details for situations that may result if one spouse eventually moves out of state.

Lawyers, of course, are not infallible. But it is very likely that they will protect the rights of both husband and wife far more effectively than either party can do through individual efforts. There is almost always more to be gained by paying an attorney than by trying to save the fees involved.

Differences in State Divorce Laws

One of the most significant differences in state divorce laws concerns residence requirements. The Supreme Court of the United States has held that every state must recognize a bona fide divorce obtained in any other state. The test is whether the state laws have been complied with at the locality where the divorce was obtained. For example, a woman living in New York may move to one of the so-called migratory divorce states and obtain a decree in no more than six weeks. A state such as New York, however, may require a period of five years' residence before a divorce may be obtained. Nevertheless, all states must recognize a divorce as valid if the judge in the place of issuance was satisfied that all state requirements for that place had been met at the time the decree was granted.

It is always possible that divorce residency requirements could be challenged, however, if the spouse seeking divorce makes statements or commits acts reflecting that he or she does not really intend to reside in the state where the divorce is sought. For this reason, lawyers sometimes recommend that the spouse filing for divorce do such things as:

1. Register to vote.
2. Obtain a driver's license, fishing license, or the like.
3. Obtain a library card as a permanent resident.
4. Transfer membership to a local church.
5. Join social clubs.
6. Lease an apartment, rather than remain on a day or weekly rate in a hotel or elsewhere.

Special Courts

A number of states now have specialized Family Law Courts, set up to handle family law problems apart from regular criminal and civil matters. For example, California has such courts in 58 counties, composed of from one to 149 departments or individual courts, each presided over by a judge of the Superior Court. Some California counties with little population have only one or two such judges. A number of the more populated counties have more than 10 judges per county (West's Annotated Government Code, Sec. 69586). These California Family Law Courts have jurisdiction to handle the following family actions and proceedings (taken from West's Annotated Civil Code, Sections 4501–4503, 4509, 4526, 4425, 4603, 196a, 231, 2650–1692, and West's Annotated Welfare and Institutions Code, Sec. 17300):

1. Dissolution of marriage (divorce).
2. Legal separation.
3. Judicial determination of void or voidable marriages (annulments).
4. Custody.
5. Child support.
6. Reimbursement of county for aid advanced to a relative.
7. Determination of paternity.
8. Proceedings under the Uniform Reciprocal Enforcement of Support Act.

A number of other states have separate courts similar to the California Family Law Courts; they handle divorce and other typical family problems. Some have similar names. In almost all of these courts, when a couple with minor children seek a divorce, the court may order conciliation meetings to attempt to resolve the matter without divorce.

Aftermath of Divorce

Frequently, the parties involved discover that there is a certain amount of legal "fall out" after the divorce, even though the matter has been officially terminated. For example, a newly divorced woman may experience difficulty in obtaining credit on her own. This is especially so if her former husband has credit problems. Too often, her credit reputation is still judged on that of her husband. Some of this problem has been solved by laws passed by Congress under Title III of the Truth in Lending Law (see Chapter 15). At times it may be necessary to obtain an attorney to clear up credit problems. A divorced woman's income may also be viewed in a different light by banks and mortgage lending institutions.

A woman in this situation may also have problems collecting

alimony, or in retaining custody of children awarded to her. The advice of an attorney may be needed in such cases.

Divorce in the Future

It is the purpose of this chapter to describe legal problems and requirements of divorce, not to be involved in social and moral considerations. But to some extent all of these problems go hand in hand.

Today, it is generally easier to obtain a divorce than in former years in most states. A certain segment of society continues to feel that divorce should never be easy to get—that making a divorce hard to obtain tends to force people to straighten out their problems. Others argue that, under society's current patterns of living, people often get married before they have matured enough to understand themselves, or to realize the "give and take" that may be involved. If people can marry so easily in almost every state, then they should be permitted the "escape route" of divorce. These observers argue that divorce should be as painless as possible. Each of the spouses experiences enough emotional trauma in obtaining the separation without having to go through a legal trauma at the same time.

In the case of *Williams* v. *North Carolina*, a husband living in North Carolina moved to Nevada with his neighbor's wife. In Nevada, the couple lived together in a trailer camp for the six-week period of residence required by Nevada law. Both then obtained Nevada divorces from their respective spouses and were then married to each other. When the couple returned to North Carolina, they were prosecuted and convicted of bigamy. This conviction was based on the assertion of North Carolina officials that the couple had not actually been divorced in Nevada, since their residence there had not been acquired in good faith. The Supreme Court held that a divorce obtained in one state must be given full faith and credit in another state and that it was up to the officials and to the courts in Nevada to decide whether the residence there was valid. Since the Nevada courts had regarded the residence as proper and had issued divorces, the North Carolina courts could not later make a determination whether the divorce was valid. Neither could North Carolina courts convict for bigamy, since the Nevada courts had already regarded the divorces as proper.

Divorce as Means of Reducing Taxes

Federal income tax rates are such that it is sometimes advantageous for a man and woman to file as unmarried individuals, rather than as married persons. Because of this situation, some couples have deliberately obtained a divorce to save taxes. One husband and wife obtained a divorce in Haiti when on vacation just before tax time. After filing individual returns, they remarried. They continued in a married state until the next year, when they again obtained a quick divorce in order to file tax returns as single individuals. The pair remarried shortly thereafter. In 1980, the Tax Court in Washington, D. C., ruled that the couple's actions had been a sham to avoid tax payments. The court assessed more than $3,000 in back taxes against the pair.

chapter 10

After the Divorce

property settlement, alimony, children

Some individuals feel that a divorce decree automatically solves all problems. The freeing of both parties may eventually come about, but divorce almost always creates problems in the areas of property settlement, alimony, support money for the children, and questions regarding child custody.

PROPERTY SETTLEMENT

Many lawyers feel that if a divorce is intended, it may be advantageous for the spouses to obtain a lawyer early enough to work out a property settlement in advance. Sometimes lawyers refer to this property settlement as a *separation agreement*. Frequently, an agreement of this kind spells out all details concerning the division of the couple's property, an arrangement for support and custody of the children, and an agreement as to the amount of alimony, if any, for the wife. From a legal standpoint, this agreement is a contract.

As we noted, the courts generally seek to uphold the institution of marriage. Courts usually hold that as a matter of public policy, they will not recognize or enforce any contract calling for the parties to obtain a divorce. Judges also usually strike down any contract or agreement by a wife to give up her right to alimony. (The courts can generally be counted on to restore a wife's right to alimony, even though she may have contracted it away in an agreement with her husband. Nevertheless, she should never sign such an agreement.)

Therefore, if a separation agreement (property settlement) is entered into by the spouses, it should be drafted by a lawyer in such a way that it may later be joined with or merged into a subsequent divorce agreement. But a separation agreement written prior to divorce cannot mention any intention to obtain a divorce; otherwise it may not be recognized by the divorce court.

If the husband and wife sign a property settlement in advance of the divorce, the judge is not bound to accept it at the time of a subsequent divorce. Generally, the judge will go along with the agreement that has been worked out if it appears to be reasonably fair (equitable) to the parties involved and to their children's interests. But from time to time a judge will alter an arrangement of this kind.

In most states, the judge presiding at a divorce trial has considerable discretion to divide property between the spouses. And in many states, the judge can later alter the terms of the alimony settlement, based on new information supplied by the husband.

A separation agreement signed prior to divorce is not always merged with the decree of divorce. In some instances, it may extend beyond the time of the divorce, serving as a private contract between the two parties, regardless of their marital status. If not incorporated into the divorce decree, the agreement cannot subsequently be changed by the divorce judge; it can be altered only by written agreement between the two parties.

ALIMONY

Alimony is the support money paid to the needy wife or husband, both during and after the divorce proceedings. Usually, alimony is a continuation of the husband's legal obligation to support the wife, an obligation assumed at the time of marriage. By law, about one-third of the states specifically exclude the husband from receiving alimony.

Other states, however, permit a needy husband to receive alimony from a well-to-do wife. Some authorities on divorce feel that all legal distinctions except that of "need" may be done away with in the future, but this may be problematical.

Under the law in a number of states following the so-called guilt or fault theory of divorce (see Chapter 9), the courts do not permit a guilty spouse to be paid alimony. A number of other states, however, permit a so-called guilty spouse to obtain alimony, even though state laws permit only exclusively fault grounds for divorce.

Where a spouse may be eligible for alimony, there is considerable variance from state to state concerning the amount that may be paid. The figure approved by the court may depend on how long the couple was married, the income potential of both parties, the age, the general health, training, and ability to work, child care responsibilities, the basic life-style to which the parties were accustomed, and other factors.

Usually, but not always, if the ex-wife wants to remarry, she will be required to give up alimony. In a few states, if the divorce is awarded because of adultery, the other spouse is not required to pay any alimony, regardless of the fact that the guilty spouse may be in real need.

Under current tax regulations, an individual receiving alimony must report payments as income; the spouse making the payments can claim them as deductions.

The fact that a court sets a specific figure for alimony does not mean that this payment may not later be changed. The courts usually look upon alimony payments as mirroring the real need of the recipient. If a destitute husband obtains a divorce and thereafter his business becomes prosperous, the wife's attorney may be able to obtain a substantial increase in alimony payments. In similar fashion, alimony payments to a divorced wife who obtains newly acquired job skills and a good job may be reduced.

It should be kept in mind that the courts in all states have the authority to modify alimony payments, according to the judge's impressions of spousal need and ability to pay. And even if regular alimony is not awarded, the courts have authority to order payment of temporary alimony, a payment that may be called *alimony pendente lite* or *suit money* in legal circles.

A rather common legal problem in recent years has been the case in which a divorced woman receiving alimony has lived as a wife with another man. Whether the courts will modify alimony payments in such a situation usually depends on the wording of the final judgment of divorce. If the divorce decree requires the husband to make alimony payments "until the ex-wife's remarriage," the courts will usually require the husband to continue alimony payments (*Josephs* v. *Josephs*, 78 Misc. 2d 723 (New York); *Sheffield* v. *Sheffield*, 310 So. 2d 410; *Rosenberg* v. *Rosenberg*, 260 N.Y.S. 2d 508). Not all courts, however, agree with this holding. If an ex-husband can satisfy the court that his ex-wife is receiving some support from a new male friend or is living with this individual, the court may reduce or eliminate alimony. It is not unusual for alimony to be cut off in a situation of this kind. Also, a woman's child does not have a right to be supported by the person the woman lives with, unless the parties get married or the woman's male companion adopts the child.

CHILD SUPPORT AND CUSTODY

Child support has nothing to do with alimony. The courts in all states insist on support for minor children. These support payments are not tied to alimony and are due whether or not the husband or wife is successful in reducing or discontinuing alimony payments. Support payments are ordinarily the responsibility of the father, regardless of who has custody. In some states, however, the mother may be required to pay if she has financial resources and the father is unable to provide support.

In a divorce action, the judge has almost unlimited discretion in deciding which parent gets custody of minor children and how visitation rights may be set. Judges with considerable experience in divorce and separation matters generally feel that mothers should be given legal custody of children, especially if the children are of tender age. In most cases, it can be expected that judges will award custody to the mother unless the father can convince the judge that the mother is incompetent or an unfit person. In many instances, the judge will order an investigative report from the court's probation officer, looking into the worthiness of each parent to be awarded custody.

In the case of *Del Pozzo* v. *Del Pozzo*, 309A. 2d 151, one of the court justices quoted the basic legal principle that is followed by practically all courts in deciding custody:

> The best interest of the child is the polestar of our law of custody as between competing parents. . . . Since the particular facts of each case are crucial to the award of custody no foolproof formula can be fashioned by which all cases can be decided. . . . Generally, a trial court bases its decision on a wide range of factors. They include the qualifications and fitness of the respective parties; their ability to control and direct the children; the age, sex, and health of the children; the environment of the proposed home and its likely influence on the children.

Cohabitation is perhaps far more common today than in former years. A number of courts take the attitude that it is damaging to the child for the mother to have a live-in relationship with a man while having custody. The courts look into these cases on an individual basis, and living together is not considered an automatic reason for revoking custody. Perhaps the majority of courts still look with disfavor at a situation of this kind, however. In the language of a recent decision (*Young* v. *Young*, 305 So. 2d 92; *Simpson* v. *Simpson*, 209 S.E. 2d 611; *Brim* v. *Brim*, 532 P. 2d 1403), the court said:

> The court being apprised that the mores and customs in regard to sexual behavior between unmarried adults where minor children resided have allegedly now become commonplace, fails to find that such alleged mores and customs and alleged common practice thereof, is conducive to the moral and spiritual well being, or proper to the welfare of the minor children. The Court further finds that the wife allowed her love for a man to diminish her fitness as a mother to her minor children, and the wife is not a fit and proper person at this time to have the care, custody and control of the minor children.

Some legal authorities feel that cohabitation by the ex-wife will not be considered in determining fitness to retain custody in the future. The majority of decided cases seem to hold otherwise, however.

Kidnapping and Child Theft from Custody

With increasing frequency following a divorce, children are being stolen from a parent having custody. Sometimes a father or mother will fail to return a child after a holiday or weekend visit. On other occasions, one parent may steal the child that is en route home from school or another activity.

Of course, if the parent perpetrating the theft can be located within the state, the judge handling the divorce and custody award will have legal jurisdiction to hold the child-stealer in contempt of court. But frequently this is not the case. A parent may kidnap a child and simply disappear without trace. The child may be taken to a distant state.

Even if the kidnapper can be located, extradition procedures and other legal dickering may be necessary to bring the offending parent back to the scene of the crime. State felony warrants may be issued, but it is usually difficult to obtain an adequate investigation at a distant location. Therefore, it may be necessary to pay for extensive private investigation to locate and return the stolen child. Your attorney's advice should be sought in a case of this kind.

At present, the Federal Kidnapping Law (sometimes called the Lindberg Law, United States Code, Title 18, Sec. 1201) specifically excepts family kidnappings from the operation of the law. The Lindberg Law was designed to apply to kidnappings for ransom or as part of another crime. But for some time, Congress has been considering a bill called the Uniform Child Custody Jurisdiction Act, which would permit all states to enforce and honor the child custody decrees of every state. Until such a Federal law is passed, the parent with rightful custody may have serious problems in the event of a kidnapping.

chapter 11

Name Changes

The courts usually say that legally a name is the identifying designation of an individual person, firm, or corporation (*Riley* v. *Litchfield*, 150 N.W. 81). A person's name is made up of one or more Christian or given names and one surname or family name (*Blakeney* v. *Smith*, 183 So. 920). And although most people believe that a child must take the father's surname, generally the courts point out otherwise:

> Custom gives one his father's name, and such praenomina (given name) as his parents chose to put before it, but this is only general rule, from which an individual may depart if he chooses (*In Re Cohen*, 255 N.Y.S. 616).

COMMON LAW RIGHT

Under the old English common law rule, a person could change his or her name to any name that was desired, so long as this change was not made for a fraudulent reason, such as to escape prosecution or to evade creditors. The courts of most states in the United States continue to recognize this right to change one's name without having to go through legal proceedings, so long as the change is not made in order to further an illegal scheme or purpose. Most other states have passed laws that provide for specified procedures to change one's name through court processes, so long as there is a reasonable purpose behind this change. In most instances, it is desirable to obtain the assistance of a local attorney in making a name change.

MARRIED WOMAN'S NAME CHANGE

There are at present no state laws that require a wife to assume her husband's surname. Nevertheless, the courts and our legal system treat a married woman as though she has automatically taken the name of the man she marries.

Some courts imply that there is a common law rule requiring a wife to take her spouse's name at the time of marriage. But this is only legal tradition or custom, and is not necessarily binding. As the judge of one federal Appellate Court said (*Forebush* v. *Wallace*, 341 F. Supp. 217):

> Certainly the custom of the husband's surname denominating the wedded couple is one of long standing. While its origin is obscure, it suffices for our purposes to recognize that it is a tradition extending back into the heritage of most western civilizations. It is a custom common to all 50 states in this union.

At one time Hawaii had a statute requiring a wife to use her spouse's name after marriage. But this law was struck down by a court decision in 1975. Puerto Rico does have a law requiring the assumption of the husband's name; Alabama reached this result by court decision (*Forebush* v. *Wallace*; affirmed per curiam, 415 U.S. 970). Attorneys General in a number of the states that have passed equal rights amendments have uniformly stated, or furnished written legal opinions that say, that the wife's assumption of her husband's name is nor required by law (according to opinions given in Alaska, Connecticut, Illinois, Massachusetts, Montana, Texas, and other states).

In the remainder of the states, there is no way of knowing how the courts might rule. Two states (Massachusetts and Minnesota) have passed laws specifically permitting a woman to continue to use her own name after marriage. In most states, it is believed that the courts would hold that usage makes any name legal, as long as the name is not used to defraud. But custom is so deeply ingrained that some state and local officials will simply not admit that usage is the controlling legal requirement. This is especially so when a married woman requests a driver's license, voting registration, or other document. If you are going to use your birth name, you should build a record of using it, getting mail, keeping a bank account or safe deposit box, and obtaining credit in your birth name.

An Arkansas court decision of 1975 was the result when four women unsucessfully attempted to register to vote. When they were not permitted to register, the women went to court and sued state officials. Two of the individuals suing (plaintiffs) were married lawyers who customarily used their birth names. A third plaintiff, named Harris, was a divorced woman who had resumed using her maiden name. The fourth plaintiff, Sister Leona Holting, was a Roman Catholic nun who wanted to be registered as a voter only as "Leona Holting." But Arkansas officials insisted that she indicate her marital status by registering as either "Miss Leona Holting" or "Mrs. Leona Holting".

Upon appeal to the Federal courts, it was held that all of the plaintiffs were entitled to be registered as they saw fit. This meant that they could use their birth names if they so desired. The court also said that the prefix requirement was unconstitutional, since it discriminated against women as a sex. Accordingly, none of the registrants was required to use the prefix "Mrs." or "Miss" (*Walker* v. *Jackson*, 391 F. Supp. 1395). The court did point out in this decision that voter registration is permanent and that changes in registration would be required if a registrant moved from one voting district to another, or if there was a change in the name of the registrant.

In the already noted *Forebush* v. *Wallace* case, which was appealed to the Federal courts, the state Driver's License Bureau was set up to issue licenses to married women, but only in their husband's names. Objecting to this procedure, a woman requested the bureau to issue a license in her birth name. Alabama officials refused to issue this license.

In this instance, the Federal court agreed with state officials. The court held that there were opposing interests here, and

> . . . that the administrative inconvenience and cost of a change to the state of Alabama . . . outweigh the harm caused the plaintiff and the members of the plaintiff's class. . . .

The court further explained that

> In balancing these interests, the court notes that the state of Alabama has (already) afforded a simple, inexpensive means by which any person, and this includes married women, can on application to a probate court change his or her name. Title 13, Sec. 278 Code of Alabama. . . .

The Federal court here also seemed to feel that the state has a legitimate interest in maintaining control over driver's license records, to avoid the possibility of anyone maintaining files under two names. The court also seemed to place emphasis on the fact that a woman could make a permanent driver's license change by utilizing the state's legal name change procedures and thereafter obtaining a license in her changed (birth) name.

Use of Man's Name in Living Together

A woman living with a man outside of marriage sometimes goes by the man's surname. When she does, the woman could possibly become involved in two kinds of unwanted legal problems: (1) if the man receives credit as a married man, the woman could be held legally responsible for his debts; and (2) if the man's surname is regularly used, the woman may legally be held to be a married woman (common law wife) in those states where common law marriages are recognized. This might be true even if the woman did not want to be considered a wife (for additional information, see Chapter 8).

CHILDREN'S NAME CHANGES

If a hospital employee makes a minor error in preparing a birth certificate, it may be corrected in most states without a court order. This is done by going to the hospital and having both the parent and the hospital employee sign an affidavit stating the nature of the error. This affidavit will usually be accepted by the state or county birth registration agency, and a new certificate will be issued upon the surrender of the original. This procedure will usually be accepted only for a minor clerical error, however. For example, the child's real name may be "Jon," although it was spelled "John" on the original birth certificate.

In some instances, parents may decide that they want to change a child's name. Usually, this can be done only by amending the original birth certificate. It is advisable to get an attorney's help in a matter of this kind.

In one case in California, a divorced woman was married for the second time, and subsequently gave birth to a son. The woman had gone to the same family doctor for many years, and the doctor was not even aware that she had remarried. In preparing the birth certificate, the doctor listed the woman's first husband as the father of the infant. This error was not discovered until several years later, when the child needed a birth certificate for school records. It was necessary for the mother to hire an attorney to go through a court procedure called a *judicial decree of paternity*. After hearing the facts, the judge almost routinely ordered the old birth record sealed and a new birth record issued. This correction, however, required the mother to spend both time and money.

chapter 12

Discrimination

jobs and promotions

In most instances today, a woman may freely work or enter the professions over the objections of her husband or family. But it was not always possible for a woman to be accepted in any kind of work. For example, in 1872, in the case of *Bradwell* v. *State of Illinois*, 83 U.S. 130, an otherwise qualified woman was denied admittance to the Illinois bar solely because she was a woman. Myra Bradwell appealed her case to the United States Supreme Court, after exhausting appeals through the Illinois courts. Bradwell's case was based on a section of the Fourteenth Amendment to the Constitution providing that "No state shall make or enforce any law which shall abridge the privileges or immunities of citizens of the United States." Bradwell maintained that both males and females are citizens, and if the privileges and immunities of a citizen cannot be abridged, then the privileges and immunities of all citizens must be the same. She also pointed out that the Illinois state regulations for admission to the bar specified that applicants must attain the age and learning required by law, and that she had met these requirements.

The Supreme Court held against Bradwell, declining to force Illinois officials to admit her to the state bar. In one of the concurring opinions in that decision, Justice Bradley of the Supreme Court said:

> Man is, or should be, woman's protector and defender. The natural and proper timidity and delicacy which belongs to the female sex evidently unfits it for many of the occupations of civil life. The constitution of the family organization, which is found in the divine ordinance, as well as in the nature of things, indicates the domestic sphere as that which properly belongs to the domain and functions of womanhood. The harmony, not to say identity, of interests and views which belong, or should belong, to the family institution is repugnant to the idea of a woman adopting a distinct and independent career from that of her husband. . . .
>
> . . . The paramount destiny and mission of woman are to fulfil the noble and benign offices of wife and mother. This is the law of the Creator.

As times changed—and despite such opinions as Bradley's—women were not to be denied. They eventually gained general (but still not total) acceptance in professional and technical occupations. But for a long time the courts and governmental agencies continued to voice the feeling that "women should be protected." In 1948, the United States in *Goesaert* v. *Cleary*, 197 U.S. 453, upheld the ruling of state authorities that a woman would not be given a state bartender's license unless she was the wife or daughter of the owner of the bar where she was to work. The reasoning was that in most circumstances a woman bartender should be sheltered against the surroundings of a bar, and this would not be possible unless her husband or father controlled activities in the place.

In recent years, women have rushed into the labor market and into the professions in great numbers. But in general, they still must accept employment in the lower paying and less challenging categories. In most types of employment, women make less money than men. And there may be significant differences when the two sexes work alongside each other at the same job, even among heads of families. Federal and state laws have started to correct some of these differences, but a wide gap still remains.

Before discussing women's employment rights in particular, it may be helpful to examine the rights of all employees, male and female.

Most employment rights and responsibilities in the United States are based on old ideas of contract law in England and Colonial America. The courts have always described employment in the private sector as "employment at will." This means that the individual or company hiring has always had the right to fire an employee at the desire of the employer. No cause need be given and no cause need exist. This is still the law when dealing with a private firm or business, unless the employee is a member of a union that has a contract with the employer. Historically, no worker has a right to be given employment or to retain a job after being hired. In the colonies, the law termed the employer "the master" and the employee "the servant."

Conditions have changed considerably in this country since colonial days, but the laws still give the employer the right to set basic terms of employment. When you take a job, the courts hold that you must obey the instructions and rules given by the employer. Undoubtedly, there are times when this insistence on adherence to instructions may work an injustice. But a business simply cannot function unless the owners and operators can operate it as they see fit, granted that they operate within the law. Consequently, employee compliance with instructions is still considered the essence of the employer-employee relationship.

The courts consistently hold that employees must be diligent in their assigned work and must take due care to make sure that their actions do not cause injury to others or loss to their employer. The courts are also in general agreement that the employer has the right to set up reasonable rules for employee activities on the job. So long as these rules are applied to all employees, or to all employees on a certain class of job, the courts will very rarely strike down such regulations.

Typical of acceptable rules are prohibitions against bringing drugs, liquor, guns, knives, or similar items into the work area, or smoking in prohibited locations. Your employer also has the right to insist that employees may not "moonlight," or work for another business in any way.

There have been no decisions by the Supreme Court on the point, but most lawyers agree that an employer may discharge an employee who does not conform to set moral standards. Thus, you could be fired because you were living together, or employment could be refused for the same reason.

Most hirings do not involve the signing of a written contract, but a contract exists, nevertheless. The law regards the employer as promising to pay a designated wage or hourly rate, with the understanding that the employee will do the work specified. If the employer does use a signed contract, it should spell out the rate of pay. Normally, an agreement of this kind will specify that the employer has the right to discharge for reasonable cause, including failure to follow instructions, dishonesty, disobedience, habitual failure to work, drinking on the job, or immoral conduct. If the employee is discharged for cause, the employer is not responsible for additional wages after that time.

Members of a union who have a labor agreement with an employer may be working under different conditions that the firm has previously agreed to. The union agreement sets out the rights of the two parties here, and they may be different from nonunion working conditions.

It should also be noted that there are a variety of laws applying to all work that children are allowed to perform and specifying conditions under which underage individuals may work. There are also a number of Federal and state laws that require employers to provide safe working conditions. These laws generally require the firm or business to warn of potential dangers and to provide adequate safety devices, tools, and techniques to prevent injury. If team safety is an element, the employer is obligated to make sure that other employees are trained in their responsibilities and job requirements.

SUPREME COURT DECISIONS

During the 1970s, Supreme Court decisions have been directed toward correcting some sexual inequalities in our laws. In *Frontero* v. *Richardson*, 411 U.S. 677, a female lieutenant in the U.S. Air Force sought increased quarters allowances and housing and medical benefits for her husband, on the grounds that he was her dependent. Such benefits are automatically granted to the wife of a male member of the armed services, but the Air Force would not make such payments to Frontero without proof that her husband was actually dependent on her for support. Frontero sued in Federal court.

The Supreme Court held that Lieutenant Frontero had been discriminated against and that there should be no differences in pay and allowance benefits between men and women in the armed forces. In this decision, Justice Brennan noted that there is stereotyped thinking in this country, "since the husband in our society is generally the 'breadwinner' in the family—and the wife typically the 'dependent' partner." Brennan's decision also pointed out:

> There can be no doubt that our Nation has had a long and unfortunate history of sex discrimination. Traditionally, such discrimination was rationalized by an attitude of "romantic paternalism" which, in practical effect, put women, not on a pedestal, but in a cage.

In *Reed* v. *Reed,* 404 U.S. 71, the Supreme Court considered the constitutionality of an Idaho state law providing that, when two individuals are otherwise equally entitled to appointment as administrator of an estate, the male applicant must be preferred to the female. The Supreme Court held this law unconstitutional, stating that it discriminated on the basis of sex and was, therefore, invalid. The court noted that there could be no "dissimilar treatment for men and women who are . . . similarly situated."

Another case of interest in the federal courts was *Diaz* v. *Pan American World Airways,* 442 F. 2d 385. In that case, male applicants for a flight attendant's job were denied employment solely because the airlines preferred female flight attendants. The Federal Appeals Court ruled that sex could not be used as a requirement since both men and women could adequately perform the stipulated duties.

CIVIL RIGHTS ACT OF 1964, AND OTHER LAWS

There are a number of significant laws and Federal administrative regulations that prohibit sex discrimination in employment. These laws and regulations include:

- The Civil Rights Act of 1964, as amended in 1972.
- Executive Order 11246, as amended by Order 11375, prohibiting discrimination in Federal contracts and Federally assisted construction projects.

- Revised Order No. 4 (1971), requiring affirmative action by Federal contractors.
- Executive Order No. 11478, prohibiting discrimination in Federal employment.
- Fair Labor Standards Act of 1938, as amended by the Equal Pay Act of 1963.
- Age Discrimination in Employment Act of 1967.
- Regulations of the Bureau of Apprenticeship and Training.

These laws and regulations add up to a confusing maze. In recent years, American law schools have often devoted a major part of labor law courses to teaching students how to interpret and file lawsuits under these laws, principally under Title VII of the Civil Rights Act. Consequently, a detailed description of the workings of this body of law is beyond the scope of this book.

In brief, Title VII of the Civil Rights Act[1] prohibits employers, labor unions, and employment agencies from discriminating in either membership or in employment on account of race, religion, national origin, or sex. Under the terms of this law, a five-member commission, appointed by the President and called the Equal Employment Opportunity Commission, was set up to handle the administration of the act.

In addition to the Federal laws that are available, most of the states and even a number of larger cities have passed additional laws prohibiting unfair employment practices. Some of these state laws and administrative regulations duplicate Title VII. State constitutional amendments also provide additional protections. The purpose of a California state law (Section 1420, California Labor Code) prohibiting discrimination on the basis of sex reads

> The purpose of the law against discrimination in employment because of sex is to eliminate the means by which persons of the female sex have historically been relegated to inferior jobs and to guarantee that in the future both sexes will enjoy equal employment benefits.

Because of the great volume of these laws, both state and Federal, a woman who is discriminated against often does not know where to turn. If the state has a fair employment agency, Federal law requires that the matter be first processed through that state agency. If

[1]The basic law is Sec. 713(b) of Title VII of the Civil Rights Act of 1964, 42 U.S. Code, Sec. 2000e-12, 78 Stat. 265.

this does not result in action on the complaint, the discrimination victim may take the matter to the Federal Equal Employment Opportunity Commission (EEOC). In some instances, lawyers recommend that the victim of sex discrimination file her complaint with both the state agency and the EEOC at the same time. If there is no state action within two months, the federal agency should then be asked to follow through.

The victim is not allowed to file a civil lawsuit for this hiring or promotional discrimination for a period of 180 days after the complaint is filed with the EEOC. Under procedural schemes that are followed, the EEOC is supposed to take no more than 180 days to investigate the facts and ascertain whether the law has been violated.

Much of the effectiveness of the EEOC comes from persuasion in its enforcement. If the EEOC is unable to persuade the employer to rectify the discrimination within an additional 30-day period, the victim of sex discrimination is entitled to receive a letter from the federal agency that authorizes a private lawsuit to be filed by the victim in federal court. This must be done within 90 days, or the right to file is lost.

TESTS FOR HIRING AND PROMOTIONS

It is almost impossible to make generalizations concerning the kinds of tests that an employer may give in evaluating an applicant's ability or a worker's eligibility for advancement. If a test results in discrimination, it must be thrown out, even though the employer may have introduced it into employment procedures in good faith. For example, a college IQ test may reflect a high level of intelligence, but it may not have any real relevance to a job driving a bulldozer. It may be relevant, however, for the city fire department to require weight-lifting tests of both male and female applicants for a firefighter's job. This is because every firefighter must be capable of dragging a smoke inhalation victim from a burning building. If a test is to be nondiscriminatory, it must call for skills or abilities that are directly related to the applicant's ability to perform the job.

In general, if job duties and requirements are the same, both men and women are entitled to equal pay. Not infrequently, a firm may give slightly different job responsibilities to a male, in order to justify unequal pay.

DISCRIMINATION AGAINST PREGNANCY

For many years in the United States, a woman was forced to take a leave of absence or was actually laid off for pregnancy in some types of jobs. Employers argued that this forced withdrawal from work was not discrimination against women, but was rather a protective act for the mother and unborn child.

Under administrative and court interpretations of United States laws, discrimination based on pregnancy is actually a form of sexual discrimination. Any loss of job rights is forbidden by these decisions and interpretations.

Medical studies show that pregnancy is not disabling to the great majority of women, and the Equal Employment Opportunity Commission has held that a woman is, therefore, entitled to stay on the job so long as she is able. The woman is then entitled to collect pay for sick leave. In addition, hospital insurance at work will often cover medical bills, but this depends on the individual policy coverage. The courts are in general agreement that a woman cannot claim disability as a result of pregnancy, unless there are some additional facts of an unusual nature.[2] Most medical authorities agree that a woman can usually return to work a short time after childbirth, if she feels like doing so.

FILING A DISCRIMINATION COMPLAINT

EEOC instructions to the public state that a complaint may be filed by an individual or group on behalf of any person who may have suffered

[2]For some views on this, see Gilbert v. General Electric, 347 F. Supp. 1058, and La Fleur v. Board of Education, 465 F. 2d 1184.

discrimination. The following steps should be taken, according to EEOC instructions:

1. Write the EEOC, asking for a discrimination charge form.
2. Fill out the form, taking all details of the alleged discrimination into account, and have it notarized.
3. File the charge as soon as possible after the discrimination occurs.
4. It is the duty of the EEOC to notify your employer of your charge. They can send an investigator to talk with you and the employer about the charge. It is unlawful for an employer to take any sanctions against an employee who has filed a complaint.
5. If the investigator feels that negotiation between employer and employee is not possible and that there is a valid charge, the EEOC can file suit in the U.S. District Court.
6. If the EEOC does not take action within 180 days after you file your complaint, you can file suit yourself.
7. Regardless of the outcome, keep accurate records and copies of all correspondence or evidence in your case until it is settled.

OBTAINING EXPERT ADVICE

Lawyers who are familiar with the problems of sex discrimination in employment almost invariably point out that the victim should obtain expert legal advice. They emphasize this point repeatedly.

Help may usually be obtained through the national headquarters of women's groups. In addition, local chapters of the National Organization for Women can assist. Through contact with women members of the bar, you may be put in contact with lawyers specializing in this field. There are also women's groups in major law schools that may be able to counsel you or to help locate suitable attorneys.

chapter 13

Women's Property Rights

Under old English law, upon marriage a husband gained control and substantial ownership rights over both his wife's personal belongings and her real estate. The wife was able only to claim the right to financial support during the existence of the marriage. Upon the husband's death, the wife had a limited right to the reversion of her own property and a limited interest in property that had been acquired during the marriage. These serious inequities were modified considerably by a series of laws passed in both England and America, called the Married Women's Property Acts. Today, some version of these laws is in force in each of the 50 states. However, there are many differences from state to state.

In all states, these laws permit a woman to retain her own individual property after marriage. In addition, the laws have some provisions that permit the woman to get and keep new property during the marriage, and under certain conditions. But the truth is that a married woman may still be at a serious financial disadvantage in a number of situations.

Because of the Married Women's Property Rights, a working woman has the right to retain her own job earnings. And she may also retain the profits, rents, dividends, or other income from her own separate property. In addition, under modern law, a husband can be convicted for stealing his wife's separate money or property (*People* v. *Morton*, 123 N.E. 2d 790). But in some states a married woman still cannot enter into a contract to make her individual property liable for debts that she wants to assume jointly with her husband. Several states prohibit a married woman from contracting to sell or lease her individual real estate without her husband's written permission. At the same time, the husband does not need her authority to sell or lease his own property. Other jurisdictions have some other restrictions on a wife's right to contract concerning her own property.

Legally, it is important for a woman to understand her property rights in specific situations and relationships that may be encountered in all areas of life. Basically, these situations divide into the following:

1. The single woman's rights to property—exactly the same as a man in purchasing, retaining, and using property. (It is only when a woman marries that problems may arise.)
2. The married woman's rights in accumulating property and in planning an estate with her husband.
3. The married woman's rights to property acquired during the marriage in the event of her husband's death.
4. The married couple's ability to pass on as much property as possible to their children or other heirs. (This, of course, involves the ability to minimize taxes.)
5. The married woman's property rights in the event of divorce or legal separation.
6. The individual woman's right to property acquired with an unmarried partner.

MARITAL PROPERTY OWNERSHIP SYSTEMS

There are two kinds of marital property ownership systems in the United States: (1) the common law state system, as it is termed in legal circles, and (2) the community property state system.

Forty-two states operate under the *common law* system and,

therefore, make up the great part of the nation. In the states that follow this system, the courts hold that a husband and wife separately own what they have purchased and paid for with their own earnings or funds. Stated in other terms, all property acquired from the husband's earnings during marriage is regarded as his property; likewise, all property bought with earnings or income of the wife is regarded as her property. Consequently, if the marriage is one in which the wife does not work, the husband is usually considered by the courts to own everything.

From the wife's standpoint, one of the basic problems here is that the husband may have legal power to dispose of all the couple's property and to retain the proceeds. All this may take place even if the wife does not agree to the sale or liquidation of the property. However, the wife in a common law state does have some legal ways to keep her husband from squandering all their resources, as we will see later in this chapter.

In *community property* states—Arizona, California, Idaho, Louisiana, Nevada, New Mexico, Texas, and Washington, as well as Puerto Rico—the basic approach is that the labor, effort, and industry of both marriage partners contributed to the acquisition of property during marriage. It is immaterial that the husband's earnings were the immediate source of most of the couple's income. Half the property acquired during marriage is, in effect, owned by each spouse. The idea is that each partner contributed to the financial success of any property acquisition, even though only one of the spouses actually had income or funds. This approach holds true even if the wife does nothing that is financially rewarding.

The only holdings not considered community property in these states consist of property that the husband or wife owned separately before marriage or inherited individually after marriage. All other property acquired after marriage is community property.

In community property states (with the exception of New Mexico), each of the marriage partners is the owner of an undivided one-half interest in the common property. Each spouse also has the power to dispose of this one-half by will, as well as the right to dispose of separate property. The courts usually say that it is immaterial which spouse's name is placed on a deed for property acquired by a couple during marriage in a community property state. It is regarded as community property if acquired during marriage.

Of course, it is possible for both spouses to own individual property in a community property state, along with the community property that is owned together. But the courts usually say that individual property must not be mingled with community funds or community property; otherwise, it becomes part of the community holdings. For example, a woman in a community property state may inherit a house and lot. So long as the deed to the property remains in her name, it is her individual property. But if she inherits $10,000 in cash and places it in a joint bank account, the cash will be regarded as community property as soon as it is mixed with money that is used by her husband. The test usually followed by the courts is whether the exact property can be traced and identified as that specific property received as the spouse's own. The courts generally allow a separate bank account to remain as individual funds.

Records of Individual Property

If a wife intends to claim that money or property belongs to her individually, it is very important that she maintain exact records of how the property was acquired and how it was paid for. The necessity to prove that individual money or property was kept segregated in a community property state has already been emphasized. And in a common law state, we have already noted that the law considers a husband and wife to own separately whatever they have independently purchased and paid for with their own funds. In a common law state, if the wife does not work the law regards the couple's income as belonging entirely to the husband. Therefore, if the couple buys a home or other piece of property, the law regards the husband as the sole owner.

But if the wife works in a common law state, she can maintain records to show that her income was used to pay for a home or other property. In this way, she can claim the home as her individual property should her husband die. Of course, the husband and wife may prefer to show that each paid for part of the property and that each spouse, therefore, owns a part that corresponds to his or her individual contribution. In a common law state, the husband's property acquisition rights are automatically taken care of if he is gainfully employed.

It should be emphasized, however, that it may be to the wife's advantage to keep detailed financial records to prove her claims of ownership. Then too, the wife may be able to support a claim of individual or part ownership by being able to prove that she used funds from an inheritance to pay for the property in question.

In addition, the wife can acquire ownership of property during the marriage by being able to show that she received funds from her husband's income as gifts and that proceeds from these gifts were used to pay off property. It may eventually be very important for the wife to be able to prove the receipt of such gifts from her husband or her relatives by written records. In some instances, lawyers recommend that the woman's husband file Federal gift tax returns with Federal tax authorities, even though the gift may not be large enough to require the payment of Federal gift taxes. The return will be documentary proof that such a gift was actually made, and it may be used eventually to establish property ownership.

Joint Ownership of Property

A woman may own property jointly with her husband or with someone else, whether the property is located in a common law state or a community property state. Married couples often favor joint ownership, since it seems to express the idea of marriage as a partnership. The relationship often promotes a sense of family harmony and unity. But there may be both advantages and disadvantages to such ownership, depending on your financial position and objectives.

Joint ownership is a legal term that is sometimes used in an inexact way. The term has many shades of meaning to the general public. Actually, there are three different kinds of joint ownership, with the owners having some different rights in each classification. If you or your husband insist on owning property together, it may be important to understand these kinds of joint ownership, due to differences in ownership, inheritance, and tax problems. The three kinds of joint ownership are called:

1. Joint tenancy, frequently known as joint tenancy with the right of survivorship (in legal circles the longer term is usually shortened).
2. Tenancy in the entirety.
3. Tenancy in common.

Joint tenancy is the most common type of joint ownership. The owners are called joint tenants in legal terminology. In most states there is no requirement that the owners must be man and wife. For example, a husband, wife, and son could all own property as joint tenants.

When one joint tenant dies the remaining joint tenant (or tenants) become owners of the whole property. This right, which accrues automatically, is called the *right of survivorship*. This legal arrangement is not dependent on state laws of descent or the existence of a will, but is owing to the nature of this kind of ownership. When property is owned in joint tenancy by a husband and wife, it is legally said that each owner has an undivided one-half interest in the entire property. If one of the owners should sell his or her undivided interest, the remaining joint tenant or tenants could receive their appropriate share by a court procedure called a *severance*.

Tenancy by the entirety is used in some states. It is quite similar to joint tenancy in every respect, except that it is limited to ownership by husband and wife. Neither can sell their individual share without permission of the other owner.

Tenancy in common is not usually used by married couples. In this form, there is no survivor who automatically takes the whole ownership upon the death of the other owner. Each owner's share passes to his or her heirs. For example, suppose you and a friend own a beach cottage as tenants in common. When you die, your half will go to your family or whomever you name in your will.

Passing on Property to Spouse Through Joint Tenancy

If a couple owns a home or other property in joint tenancy, we know that the ownership will pass to the survivor upon the death of one of the partners. This, of course, is an arrangement frequently used in all states. One of its features is that it takes the property out of probate. The surviving wife automatically owns the family home in a situation of this kind, whether or not the husband leaves a will. Consequently, joint tenancy is often a desirable kind of ownership, especially if the couple intends to pass on as much property as possible to a surviving wife or husband.

But joint tenancy, if not properly planned, could cause problems. As previously emphasized, in common law states the courts hold that a husband and wife separately own whatever they have independently purchased with their own funds. A husband may intend to leave the family home to his wife by placing the ownership in joint tenancy during his lifetime. But unless the wife can show that her funds were used to pay off this property, she may not be able to establish ownership after her husband's death, even though the title was held in joint tenancy. If the wife can establish that she paid for the property with gifts from her husband, then she may avoid a subsequent property ownership dispute. Then too, it may be desirable for the husband to leave the home to his wife by will. But when this technique is used, the husband's estate may be liable for some expensive Federal estate tax assessments.

This discussion is designed merely to outline some of the problems that could arise in estate planning. Consequently, if a married woman and her husband are attempting to accumulate and pass on as much property to the other as possible, it is usually advisable to work out a plan that fits the legal requirements of their state of residence. Although most of us are somewhat hesitant to contact an attorney unless we are in trouble, legal assistance is almost invaluable in planning the best way to accumulate money or property.

Passing on Property to Children or Other Heirs

After working out a plan to care for a surviving spouse, the next problem may be to decide how to pass on as much property or money as possible to children or other heirs, after the death of both marriage partners. Our inheritance laws and our estate tax laws are set up so that a couple cannot accomplish both objectives. That is, if the husband passes on the maximum amount to his widow, the couple will not be able to pass on the maximum inheritance to the couple's children or other heirs.

In actual practice, however, it may be possible for an attorney to set up a trust as part of the inheritance of the widow, using this legal device to pass on a maximum inheritance to the couple's children. This is a matter for an attorney who is well versed in trust and estate problems. In setting up a plan to accumulate as much as possible, it is often worthwhile to consult a lawyer who handles such matters.

Estate Tax Problems

Without obtaining legal advice, many couples automatically put all their savings and investments into joint ownership. One of the legal problems here is that putting title in joint ownership does not exempt the property from the Federal estate tax when one of the partners dies. Under Federal court decisions, internal revenue authorities treat the value of the entire piece of jointly owned property as a taxable asset owned by the first of the joint owners to die. Internal revenue authorities do, however, permit the survivor to prove that the deceased did not pay for all of the property. Estate taxes will not be assessed against that fractional part paid for by the survivor. In most instances, however, married couples have so intermixed their funds that it is almost impossible to show who actually made the payments on jointly owned property. Then too, in many families the husband makes the payments on the home or other property and takes care of essentials. If the wife works, she may use her money for clothing, the children's expenses, vacations, and luxuries that are used for the entire family.

The truth is that in many instances both spouses contributed to the payment of jointly owned property. If the husband dies first and the wife's contributions cannot be proved, the entire property will be subject to the Federal estate tax. The value of this same property will probably also be taxed a second time when the second spouse dies, leaving the property to the couple's children. Estate planners point out that in such instances double taxation can result from joint ownership of family property.

Avoiding Joint Tenancy in a Second Marriage

Ownership of an entire piece of property passes to the surviving spouse when the property is owned in joint tenancy. Consequently, a couple in a second marriage may not want to own a home or other property in joint tenancy. If both spouses have financial independence as a result of a prior marriage, individual ownership should be considered. If the wife has children of her own by a prior marriage, her children will probably eventually gain title to the jointly owned property. This arrangement, of course, would cut out the offspring of the second husband, if he died before the wife.

From the estate planning standpoint, it may be advantageous for a couple to switch from joint ownership of property to individual ownership of one-half by each spouse. But a decision of this kind could increase liability for estate taxes, gift taxes, and income taxes. Change in the type of ownership by a married couple should not usually be considered without first obtaining the advice of an attorney.

Protecting Wife's Property in a Common Law State

If a wife does not work, as we know, the courts in a common law state treat the couple's income as belonging entirely to the husband. If the husband uses this income to buy property and pay for it, he has the right to thereafter dispose of the property as he sees fit. The husband may fritter away the proceeds or hide the money from his wife. It is possible in some instances for the husband to leave the wife penniless. There are, however, some legal devices for the wife's protection in a number of states, such as the right of dower.

For hundreds of years under the old feudal system in England, the property was all owned by the crown. Gradually, the common people wrested from the monarch the right to own real estate and make wills, disposing of that which they owned. Some husbands, in time, found it "inconvenient" to provide for their widows. This problem eventually caused such concern that the English Parliament and courts worked out the legal principle that is called the *right of dower*.

Under this rule, the courts held that a surviving widow was automatically entitled to a "life estate" in one-third of any real estate or tract of land that her husband had owned at any time during their marriage. Most of the wealth in early England was represented by farms and rental property. This meant that the widow had a right to occupy, rent out, farm, or use one-third of the land that had belonged to her husband. This life estate interest lasted as long as the widow lived. She could charge a tenant farmer for land rental, collect money from homes or apartment units, or use the property in any way that did not destroy the value or substance. Of course, the widow's interest ended when she died, but it kept her provided for in many instances, even if her husband attempted to disown her.

In community property states, there is no real need for dower and so the principle does not apply there. The right still exists in a substantial number of common law states, however. In such jurisdictions, such as in the Midwest, the dower right has been increased to give the widow a life estate in one-half of the husband's lands, rather than a life estate in one-third of such property. In some other common law states, the dower right has been modified or done away with.

It should be noted that the dower right applies to land or real estate only, not to such property as stocks and bonds, bank accounts, or corporate interests. Because of this limitation, dower sometimes does not work as well today as it did in rural England. Although a life interest in real estate is usually valuable, much of the wealth in the United States is now in trust funds, bank accounts, and other forms of assets. There is always the possibility in some states that a wealthy man who owned no real estate could leave his wife near penniless if she was disinherited in his will.

Lawyers for the purchaser of real estate in a common law state usually insist that the wife sign away her dower right in property, even though the husband is the sole owner. Of course, if the wife declines to sign, it is unlikely that the buyer will be interested in the property.

Statutes in a number of common law states give a surviving wife a choice between her dower right and any money or property that may have been left to her in her husband's will.

In some common law states, a surviving husband has the right of *curtesy*, which corresponds generally to the right of dower. Under the law in most jurisdictions, the right of curtesy does not come into being unless the couple had children.

If a husband had a company retirement plan, some common law states take the position that the wife's rights as a beneficiary may be vested, or fixed, and that a disinherited wife had a specified interest in company pension rights, in spite of the fact that the husband attempted to disinherit her in his will. At any rate, this possibility for uncovering assets should not be overlooked in the event of the husband's hostility.

Wife's Right to Share in Husband's Estate

A number of states now have statutes providing that any transfer of real estate by a husband within two years of his death is regarded as a fraud on his wife, and the dower right in such property can be claimed by the widow as though the husband still owned this real estate at the time of his death. In effect, this sometimes works against a husband's efforts to sell off real estate and hide the proceeds from his wife. It is also worth noting that there are now laws in all but seven of the common law states giving a surviving spouse a fixed percentage of the value of the deceased husband's assets, in spite of any attempt he may have made to disinherit her by will. Laws of this kind vary, usually allowing the surviving wife from one-third to one-half of the value of the husband's estate.

Forced Heirship Laws

So-called *forced heirship laws* have been passed in both common law and community property states. These laws specify that a set percentage of any individual's estate must be left to specific heirs, usually a wife and/or children. In the event the maker of the will has no heirs that qualify, the legal requirement does not, of course, apply. Where laws of this kind are in effect, the surviving wife, children, or husband who qualifies has the option of taking under the terms of the will or under the heirship statute, obtaining whichever is the greater amount.

The courts usually hold that forced heirship statutes apply only to such property as was owned at the time of death. Thus, in extreme cases it would be possible to sell property and secrete the proceeds, or give it away, thereby cutting off the rights of the deceased's survivors.

PROPERTY RIGHTS IN DIVORCE

It is impossible to generalize concerning a wife's property rights in the event of a divorce. In most of the states in the United States today, the trial court judge has almost absolute discretion to divide the property accumulated by both parties during the marriage in a way the judge believes fair to both. The name on the deed to property is not controlling on the court. The family home or any other piece of property in the husband's name may be given to the wife. In some instances, attorneys point out that a woman who can document the real worth of her husband's assets may have an easier time in convincing a court of what property should be awarded to her in a divorce settlement.

Antenuptial Agreements

An *antenuptial agreement* is a contract drawn up to retain individual property so that a future husband or wife will not have control over it. Usually, an arrangement of this kind is used when either a man or a woman with considerable property is entering into a second marriage. Although less common today, it is still utilized, especially in community property states. The advice of an attorney is suggested with a device of this kind.

PROPERTY RIGHTS WITH AN UNMARRIED PARTNER

Usually, unmarried people living together have no right to property acquired by the other individual while living together. In some instances, a woman companion may be able to claim property on the basis of a contract relationship, but community property principles cannot be used by the courts to award half the property acquired by a live-in partner. This problem is discussed in more detail in connection with the case of *Marvin* v. *Marvin* in Chapter 8.

The courts almost always hold that persons living together have no right to sue for injuries sustained by the other, regardless of the fact that the injury was negligently or wrongfully inflicted.

chapter 14

Renting Rights

Singles, young marrieds, and couples subject to transfer generally expect to rent, rather than buy a home or apartment. Others may rent for extended periods through choice or because of high housing costs.

There are both practical and legal advantages and drawbacks in renting or leasing. Many people feel that it is enjoyable to be freed from time-consuming maintenance tasks. On the other hand, non-owners may be subject to alarming rent increases. And there is always the possibility of problems if the landlord does not correct maintenance deficiencies.

The landlord's responsibilities vary from locality to locality, depending on a multitude of local city ordinances and health and building codes. The individual you rent from may be the owner. But in metropolitan areas, this person is frequently a representative of a management or real estate firm that operates the building and serves as an agent for the owner. The person who rents to you generally has the authority to commit the owner, and this agent's dealings are legally considered those of the owner. In any event, both the owner (landlord) and the renter have legal responsibilities to each other.

Landlords and renters frequently have difficulties and misunderstandings. But usually these can be worked out if both sides act reasonably. It is not uncommon, however, for either party to fail to understand what their rights consist of.

As a renter, your rights are more limited than they would be if you owned the property. In some respects, the owner still has more rights than the renter. But tenants have certain rights, also, that cannot be taken away.

MONTH-TO-MONTH TENANT

When you pay rent by the month, you are called a *month-to-month tenant*. Under the laws in most states, you have the right to stay on month after month until the landlord gives you 30 days' notice to vacate. Unless there are rent control laws that apply, the landlord can raise the rent at any time, effective 30 days after notice is given. The law in most states gives the landlord the right to move you out and take repossession of the property after giving 30 days' notice. If you do not move after this time, the landlord can have you evicted by the sheriff.

ADVANTAGES OF A LEASE

Sharply rising rent rates in recent years have emphasized some of the economic and legal problems of renting. Tenants are too often at a disadvantage in times of economic inflation. Consequently, the time for a renter to consider self-protection is before moving into a rental unit. A written contract with the landlord for a specified amount of rent payment solves this problem for the duration of the contract agreement. This type of contract, of course, is a *lease*. But while the landlord cannot raise the rent during the term of the lease, neither can the tenant move out and quit paying the regular monthly payments.

A lease is subject to whatever conditions the renter and the landlord agree to. If the tenant is likely to be transferred to a distant job location, it is usually advisable for the tenant to have the option to cancel the lease. Otherwise, he or she must continue the payments.

Often, a lease requires the payment of some fee if you are late in rental payments. It is well to keep in mind that when you sign a lease you are making a contract, and it must be regarded as such. Both the renter and the landlord are legally bound by all the requirements set out in this agreement. It is also worth noting that most printed lease forms were originally drawn up for landlords, and they almost invariably favor the landlord's interests.

When you are working out arrangements on a new rental, the landlord or manager handling the property will sometimes give you a printed lease form, stating that it is "the usual or standard type." Regardless of what the landlord says, you should read this form in great detail before placing your signature on it. This is in spite of the fact that the form may be printed in fine print and may be quite lengthy. If you do not agree to all or some of the provisions, you should write out an attachment or addition to the form, specifying the provisions agreed to. This written part should appear on all copies and should be signed at the end by both parties to the agreement. If some parts of the lease are struck through, these parts should be carefully marked out in ink and initialed on all copies by both tenant and landlord. The rental agent may handle this responsibility for the landlord, if the property has been left in the hands of an agent.

The legal formalities for preparing a lease vary from state to state. In most jurisdictions, a lease for less than one year may be handled by a verbal agreement, but a rental for a year or more requires a written document. It is almost always advisable to have a written lease if the tenant intends to stay for more than a few months.

There are still some states, mostly in the East, where a lease must be prepared with the same formal requirements used to prepare a deed for the sale of land. A few states still require a lease to be drawn up with a formal wax seal, and a number of states require a lease to be signed by witnesses and/or notarized, or formally acknowledged.

Lawyers also point out that it may sometimes be advisable to have a lease recorded with the office of the county recorder. Usually, this procedure is followed only for leases of business and industrial tracts. But it is recommended if there is any question concerning the credit or financial standing of the landlord.

In checking the suitability of a lease, it is suggested that the renter consider the following:

1. The identity and signatures of the parties who will be responsible for performance of lease requirements. If the tenants are married, some landlords ask both husband and wife to sign as responsible for payments under the lease. With a requirement of this kind, some legal advisers state that both the landlord and the landlord's spouse should also be required to sign.

2. The amount of monthly rent payments and the due date. Penalties that may be due for late payments should also be specified. If all monthly rent payments automatically fall due in case of tenant default, these terms should be spelled out in detail. Usually, it is not desirable for the tenant to sign a provision of this kind, unless the rental will not otherwise be made available.

3. A provision that the lease may be canceled if the renter is transferred by his or her employer, or if the renter accepts employment at a distant location.

4. Responsibility for repairs and the payment of utilities should be clearly specified.

5. The number of individuals permitted to occupy the premises should be included, along with a statement that the premises may be sublet to another renter in the event the tenant decides to move out during the lease period.

6. Provisions for a security and cleaning deposit may be included, if such deposits are required by the landlord. If one month's rent must be deposited, this should also be specified.

7. The landlord's right of entry should be described.

8. Conditions under which the tenant could make additions or changes to the premises should be listed.

There are a number of other options that a renter may want to have included in a lease contract. For example, there are times when a building is harmed by fire, but an apartment is still intact. In a situation of this kind, the renter's apartment may have little practical value, since outside facilities in the building are unusable. To avoid this possibility, the tenant may insist on a provision that rent will not be due if facilities in the building are seriously affected by fire, earthquake, or other catastrophe or condition.

In addition, there are some states that still follow the old English idea that rent would be due even if the building should be destroyed by fire or catastrophe. Renters should, therefore, consider a provision that they will not be liable for rent payments if the building becomes unusable.

TENANT/LANDLORD RIGHTS AND RESPONSIBILITIES

Responsibility for Repairs

Under old English law, the landlord had no duty to make repairs or keep the property in working order. Today, laws vary somewhat from state to state, but local city codes usually require the landlord to be responsible for basic repairs. Of course, if the tenant breaks a window or misuses the property, it is still up to the renter to put the property back in usable condition.

At the time you rent or lease, it is always advisable to have a definite understanding with the landlord concerning who will be responsible for repairs. Preferably, this statement should be placed in writing if there is a question in your mind.

There are still a few states where the tenant accepts the property in the condition under which it is first occupied. More and more, however, states are turning to a legal principle called the *requirement of habitability*. In simple terms, this means that it is the landlord's responsibility to furnish a place that is habitable, or liveable, in every way, but not necessarily luxurious. If the renter did not detect that the sewer system was not functioning properly at the time the occupancy began, it is still the landlord's legal responsibility to make the sewage system work. Under this idea of habitability, most courts hold that the landlord must provide a place that is reasonably clean and acceptable to local sanitation and health codes, that is vermin-free, that has adequate water, heat, light, garbage pickup, workable windows and doors, functioning locks, elevators and stairways, and air conditioning where furnished.

Usually, habitability requirements pertain to low cost housing, but this principle has been applied to all classes of rental property. For example, a court in the Midwest recently allowed tenants in a luxury building to deduct the cost of rented air-conditioners when the permanent installation failed to function after reasonable notice to the landlord.

The courts often speak of this habitability requirement as a *warrant of habitability* by the landlord—in short, a guarantee of habitability. How this right may be enforced varies from state to state. If you have a legitimate claim concerning habitability, it is usually advisable to contact the landlord by telephone with a request for repairs. If nothing happens, it is then usually best to notify the landlord by a letter sent by registered mail. The tenant should keep a copy of this written request, stating the problem in simple terms and asking for action.

If nothing happens, the problem may then be reported to city or state authorities, who may be able to take some action on your behalf. For example, if the landlord stops the garbage pickup service, the city health inspector may be able to force action to correct the problem.

In some instances, it may be advisable for the tenant to file suit against the landlord in small claims court. This usually costs only a minimum filing fee and frequently is worth the time involved. In most states, you do not need an attorney to file a claim of this kind. Usually, the tenant goes into small claims court and relates that the landlord took no action when requested. The judge then awards damages to the tenant unless the landlord can present evidence that the property owner was not responsible. The procedures in small claims court are usually very informal. The clerk of any local or state court listed in the telephone book can usually direct you to the appropriate small claims court. Once at this location, you can generally depend on the clerk of the small claims court for advice on filing and on how to present your case.

There are other legal actions that you can take if your landlord refuses to make the place habitable or fails to make necessary repairs. In some states, you can make the repairs yourself and deduct these costs from your next rent check. In other states, the renter may simply withhold rent payments until the landlord makes proper repairs. In all localities, you can obtain an attorney and begin a lawsuit, requesting damages from the landlord.

Deducting rent or withholding rent is not advisable, however, unless the landlord has agreed in advance, or unless you are acting on the advice of an attorney. In most states, the landlord is entitled to receive full rent from the tenant under all circumstances and can evict if full rent is not paid on time. Usually, attorneys recommend that you try to work out differences on a face-to-face basis with the landlord, rather than to withhold rent. Lawyers point out that it may be better for you to take a photograph or two of the condition in dispute and to, thereafter, get a judgment in small claims court. The judgment obtained can then be offset against the rent that is due.

If a renter does not want to pursue his or her claim in small claims court, it may be advisable to consult a private attorney. During this conference, the attorney will sometimes point out that the matter can be pursued for less cost if the tenant is willing to handle the matter in small claims court. If the tenant is unable to pay for regular attorney's fees, legal help may be obtained through a telephone call to the local legal aid office. The number for legal aid can usually be obtained by a telephone call to any attorney's office.

What Landlords Can Expect

Renting gives the tenant the right to use property as if he or she owned it. But there are differences. The tenant does not have a right to remove built-in book cases, change walls, or make permanent alterations, even if these changes improve the appearance and increase the value of the property. It is the tenant's basic responsibility to keep the rental in the same condition as when occupancy was granted. Of course, there will always be deterioration from normal use and wear, but if the tenant tears up the premises, rips out the wallpaper, or defaces the woodwork beyond normal use, the occupier must pay for such damage.

If you want to alter the property to your own artistic taste, permission to do so should be obtained in writing. Otherwise, you can anticipate that the landlord may evict you or sue for damages. This may be difficult to swallow, especially if you can see that alterations could improve the premises. Nevertheless, this responsibility to vacate in substantially the same condition is the law in all localities. In addition, the tenant has the legal responsibility to keep the property reasonably clean. Gas, electrical, and plumbing connections must be used only as intended. And a tenant has no right to delay payment of rent. To do so could lead to eviction.

Renter Security Deposits

The withholding of security deposits is a frequent cause of friction between renters and landlords. There is always a certain amount of wear in a rental unit, and the security deposit cannot be used to take care of normal use or deterioration. The landlord has, however, the right to use the security deposit to change alterations in the premises made by the renter, even if the unit is left in spotless condition.

Some landlords wrongfully feel that they have the right to keep the security deposit as a bonus to the rent money, even though the property was vacated substantially as rented. Because of landlord abuses, a number of states passed laws in the 1970s specifically stating that deposits cannot be retained to cover reasonable wear and tear on rental units. Most of these state laws also specified that the landlord could not disguise the nature of the renter's deposit by calling it an administrative fee, a key deposit, a pet deposit, an advertising fee, preparation fee, or other name. Usually, these laws also specify that the deposit cannot exceed one month's rent.

A demand for return of the renter's deposit should be made immediately before vacating the premises, with a request that the landlord or rental agent examine the property in person. If the deposit is not returned, a call should be made to the city or state rental association, as well as the landlord's attorney, if known. If there is still no action, a complaint should be immediately filed in small claims court, and the owner subpoenaed to appear. Some state laws now permit the renter to recover the deposit plus some additional damages as a penalty against landlords who abuse the deposit privilege. The clerk of the small claims court can usually advise a renter of additional damages that may be asked for.

Right of Unmarried Couple to Rental

A landlord can usually refuse to rent to an unmarried man and woman, solely because of the fact of the unmarried relationship. This is because cohabitation or fornication (sexual intercourse between unmarried persons) is a crime in most states. If the landlord is aware of the fact that the couple is unmarried, he or she could be prosecuted for aiding, abetting, or facilitating a crime. In jurisdictions where cohabitation and fornication are not regarded as crimes, the unmarried couple have the right to obtain a rental. In most instances, the landlord has considerable discretion in deciding whether the prospective tenant would be desirable as a renter. A lawsuit to force the landlord to provide a rental would seldom be worth the money and time involved, from a practical standpoint.

Working a deception on the landlord by misrepresenting the fact that the couple is unmarried could make the tenants liable for fraud in some states, if the landlord thereby suffers monetary damage.

Landlord Rights

In recent years, some renter's rights groups have implied that the renter's rights are superior to those of the landlord. But both tenants and landlords have rights that must be respected.

Once the property has been rented, certain rights cannot be taken away from the tenant. But there are no legal requirements that force a landlord to rent property in the first place. And if it is rented, there is no way that you can compel the landlord to make the rental available to you. Of course, there are laws that prohibit a landlord from discriminating because of race, color, or religion. But the owner still has the right to decide whether the property will be used as a rental or withdrawn from the rental market, and whether the property will be turned over to a specific individual. Property laws give the landlord the right to use property as deemed fit by that owner, so long as rent control and discrimination laws are not violated. The landlord can refuse to rent to you if it appears that you have inadequate income or are a poor financial risk. You may also be turned down if you have a reputation for causing damage, making excessive noise, or conducting a business on rental premises in violation of city codes. And in most instances, owners have a right to convert existing rental units into condominiums.

There are variances in the laws from state to state, but usually the landlord has the right to come in and inspect the property and check for needed repairs. Generally, an entry is allowed in these instances:

1. To make necessary or already agreed upon repairs, to repaint or redecorate, to supply necessary equipment and maintenance, to install improvements.
2. To take care of an emergency, such as a broken water pipe.

3. To let in real estate sales people, buyers, new tenants, or repairpersons when the tenant is surrendering occupancy.
4. To examine and repair property when the tenant has vacated, even though the rental period may not yet have terminated.

RENT CEILING LAWS OR ORDINANCES

Because of frequent rent increases, a number of cities have passed rent ceiling laws. Many of these laws provide jail terms for landlords who demand rent increases beyond designated ceilings. A considerable number of lawyers feel that at least some of these rent control ordinances eventually will be held unconstitutional, since their effect is to deprive the owner of the right to manage and control private property.

A number of cities have also passed laws restricting the conversion of rental apartments into condominiums. Here again, some attorneys feel that at least some of these anticonversion ordinances eventually may be held unconstitutional. Some of the legal aspects of rent control and condominium conversion may not be settled for a number of years, following appeals to the Supreme Court.

LIABILITY AS A TENANT

As a tenant, you may be legally responsible for injuries incurred by outsiders who are on the premises. It is sometimes hard to determine whether this responsibility is that of the owner of the premises or that of the person in control of the property through a rental or lease arrangement. Generally, the legal test of responsibility turns on two questions: (1) whether the landlord had the premises in a safe condition when the occupancy began, and (2) whether the landlord continued to have maintenance responsibility under the rental or leasing agreement.

If the tenant and the landlord had an agreement whereby the landlord would continue to be responsible for maintenance and repairs, the courts in most states will hold the landlord responsible for injury to an outsider. But if the premises were safe when turned over, and if the tenant agreed to keep up repairs, the landlord would not be held responsible for outside injuries by most courts.

RETALIATORY EVICTION

As we are aware, landlords may evict for nonpayment of rent, for destruction or serious alteration of property, or because the tenant lives in such a way that other tenants are greatly disturbed in their use and enjoyment of the property. These reasons are all considered legally justified.

In some situations, however, a landlord may evict merely to strike back at a tenant who has reported some of the landlord's derelictions or lapses of responsibility to state or local authorities. An eviction of this kind is known in legal circles as a *retaliatory eviction*. Under the law as interpreted by the courts for hundreds of years, the landlord needed no reason of any kind to evict after giving the required legal notice. Today, however, a great many state courts are refusing to permit an eviction where the only reason is to "settle a grudge" or "to get even with a tenant."

In the usual case of this kind, the tenant is evicted after complaining to state or local authorities about an unsafe or unsanitary building code violation. In this situation, the court's reasoning is that the tenant would never come forward to report legal violations unless given some protection.

From a practical standpoint, one of the legal difficulties in proving a retaliatory eviction is to convince the court of the landlord's real intent. A number of states have passed laws specifying a legal presumption of wrongful intent by the landlord who evicts within 60 days after a tenant has complained of the landlord's code violation to authorities. If a tenant has given the landlord some legitimate cause to evict, the landlord may be able to convince the court that an eviction was not prompted by retaliation for reporting a code violation.

chapter 15

Women and Credit

Credit is a convenience that allows you to enjoy the use of money, property, or goods before you have paid for them completely. If you buy a car or house on credit, you enjoy all the privileges of ownership from the beginning, even though it may take you several years of regular monthly time payments to repay the lender in full. (This chapter does not cover mortgages, real estate, or houses; see Chapter 13.)

If you have ever charged goods at a department store or used a credit card to pay for gas, you have taken advantage of the convenience of credit. And if you have ever been surprised at how much finance charges increase your total bill, or discovered at the end of a month that you have overextended yourself by charging goods you really cannot afford to pay off, you know some of the dangers of credit, too. It is possible today to charge almost any goods or service. Although this may make life easier, the wise consumer will use credit sparingly and will investigate how much finance charges and interest will increase the cost of an item before signing any credit agreement or using a credit card.

When you apply for credit, your prospective creditor wants to be reasonably sure that you will make your payments regularly and on time. Over the years, creditors have developed an elaborate system of "scoring" potential customers. Working with your application, your creditor decides whether people with similar characteristics, income, and so on have paid their bills promptly in the past. The creditor considers three main factors called the "Three C's of Credit"—capacity, collateral, and character.

Capacity means that creditors want to know if you have the means to repay the loan out of your immediate income. On the application, you will be asked to give the name of the company you work for, how long you have worked there, and how much money you make. If your job is seasonal or if you work in a company whose future is uncertain, you may not be considered a good credit risk. On the other hand, if the creditor determines that you have a steady income or the potential to increase your income through raises or promotions, you are more likely to receive credit.

Creditors also want to know how much of your income is likely to be immediately available to repay bills. They will ask how many dependents you have to support and whether you already have heavy obligations to other creditors.

Collateral means your financial assets other than income. An immediate capacity to pay bills is a good indication that you deserve credit, but a creditor also wants to be sure that you have a secondary source of funds, in case illness or sudden unemployment depletes your immediate income. This secondary source, or collateral, could be property, savings, or stocks and bonds that could be converted to ready money to repay your bills. A creditor will ask you to list any property you own or are paying for, any stocks you own, and any savings accounts that hold money.

Character is important to creditors in determining if you take financial obligations seriously. They will check with your other creditors to see if you pay your bills on time, or if you have already borrowed more than you can reasonably expect to repay on your salary. They will also ask if you rent or own your home, and how long you have lived there. Rightly or wrongly, creditors generally feel that a person who owns a house and has lived there for years is more stable and more likely to repay bills than a person who rents, especially if she changes apartments every few months.

IMPROVING YOUR CREDIT

Unless you have never applied for credit, you already have a "credit history"—a file of information about your job, previous bills, how you handled them, and so on. This file is kept at a local credit agency and is available only to you and to prospective creditors, who use the information to determine if you are a good "credit risk."

If you have decided that you want to create your own credit history so that you are able to borrow money in the future, there are several ways to begin.

1. Start checking and savings accounts in your own name. This does not actually give you a credit history, but if your bank is able to report that you maintain or increase your balances and do not overdraft your account, creditors are likely to see you as reliable.

2. Apply for a bank credit card or a checking account with an automatic "line of credit." Many banks offer good customers a bank card; it allows you to charge purchases. However, if you do not repay the amount you have borrowed within a specified period—usually about a month—you will be charged interest. Banks that offer credit through a checking account allow you to write a check for more than your actual balance. Here again you have a limit, but in this case you automatically pay interest, since the bank regards the money you have borrowed as a loan.

3. Open your own charge account at a retail store. Apply in your own name. You will be given a specific amount, which is your "limit," or the total dollar amount that you are allowed to charge. For instance, if your limit is $100, you can charge $100 worth of camping equipment, but you canot charge anything else until you have paid for some of your camping gear. If you pay the store $25 of your bill, you can now charge up to $25 worth of goods; but at no time can you have an unpaid balance of more than $100. If you have no previous credit history, your limit will be low. And remember, if you open a charge account specifically to improve your credit record, pay your bills as soon as you receive them, if possible. Otherwise, you may be charged a percentage of your bill as interest—up to 18 percent in many states. In addition, paying immediately will impress prospective creditors with your reliability.

4. Applying for a small loan sometimes can be a good way to build

your credit rapidly. Here, a borrower does not actually intend to use the money she borrows. Instead, she puts it in a separate savings account and repays it regularly and promptly. Even though you lose money in the long run—you will be charged interest for your loan—a credit bureau will later report your good repayment record to other lenders.

5. If you are married and share your husband's credit accounts, write to all the creditors and ask them to report your credit in both names, yours and your husband's. (If you are listed as Mrs. John Doe, the account will continue to be in his name only, but if you ask the creditors to report your history as Mary Doe, you will be given a separate file.) Also ask the creditors to send you new cards in your own name.

6. Have a utility or phone bill put in your own name and pay the bill regularly and in full. This is more evidence that you handle financial matters responsibly.

The Equal Credit Opportunity Act

At one time, it was especially difficult for women to obtain credit. Lenders assumed that single women had low incomes, or would eventually marry. And they made it difficult for a married, widowed, or divorced woman to get credit in her own name, on the assumption that men usually controlled women's finances anyway. The Equal Credit Opportunity Act of 1975 (ECOA), however, gives everyone the right to be considered for credit. ECOA does not, of course, insure that all women will automatically receive credit, but it does make it much easier for women to prove their credit worthiness. Since the passage of ECOA, it is illegal for creditors to discriminate against anyone because of sex, age, religion, race, national origin, or marital status. And creditors cannot ask a woman applicant questions that they would not ask a man, or refuse credit to a woman if they would extend it to a man in identical circumstances.

So, there are a variety of questions a creditor *cannot* ask you when you apply for an individual account in your own name.

- A creditor cannot specifically ask your sex (unless you are applying for a home loan, in which case the government requires the creditor to ask your sex. But even so, you do not have to supply the information). Obviously, if you are face-to-face with your creditor, sex can generally be determined without having to ask.

- A creditor cannot ask your marital status when you apply for an individual account—a retail credit card, bank credit card, and so on—unless you live in a community property state (Arizona, California, Idaho, Louisiana, Nevada, New Mexico, Texas, and Washington, as well as Puerto Rico). If you do live in a community property state, a creditor can ask if you are married, unmarried, or separated. Creditors have no right to ask if you are divorced or widowed.
- A creditor cannot ask if you have your own phone; this qualification would exclude married women.
- A creditor cannot ask if you plan to have children or inquire about your birth control practices. Nor can creditors simply assume that you plan to have children.
- Unless you live in a community property state, a creditor cannot ask questions about your husband or ex-husband, unless the alimony he pays will be a source of your financial support.
- A creditor cannot automatically require your husband to cosign a loan application, unless you live in a community property state. In some cases, a bank or other creditor will refuse credit or a loan unless the prospective customer can find a cosigner. This happens frequently when someone with a short credit history applies for credit; the bank protects itself by requiring a financially established person to cosign the application. Your cosigner is liable for your debts if you do not pay them. If you are married and need a cosigner, you do not automatically have to get your husband to sign. A relative, friend, or business associate who meets the creditor's standards of credit worthiness must be accepted.
- A creditor cannot legally discourage you from applying for credit by implying that you are unlikely to get it anyway, nor can a creditor delay your application to discourage you.

You have no legal obligation to circle Miss, Ms., or Mrs. on a credit application.

Special Problems in Establishing Credit

Before 1977, a woman who was or had been married often had trouble establishing her own credit. Now, the situation is somewhat simpler, thanks to the Equal Credit Opportunity Act. Previously, women did not share their husbands' credit histories, so a newly divorced woman or a widow often found her credit cancelled suddenly. When she reapplied for credit, her application was frequently denied—because she had no credit record in her own name. ECOA provides that, if your joint account was opened after June 1, 1977, you share your husband's credit history for that account. Now, a widow or newly divorced woman can apply for credit, and the creditor will examine the couple's joint credit record. If it was good, the prospective creditor will view her application more favorably, although, of course, the joint credit record is not the only factor that will guide the prospective creditor to grant credit. A woman also needs to show that she has the current capacity and collateral to repay bills.

The ECOA is not automatically retroactive, however, and if you have a joint charge account that was opened before June 1, 1977, it could be cancelled if your husband died or you were divorced. But if you ask your mutual creditors, they will put their reports to the credit bureau in both spouses' names, no matter when the account was started.

Of course, if a husband and wife sharing joint accounts have a bad credit history, the woman shares that, too. Today, increasing numbers of married women choose to keep their bank accounts, checking accounts, and credit cards in their own names and pay their bills from their own incomes.

Income Sources for Credit Eligibility

Before ECOA, some divorced women discovered that their credit applications were rejected because their sole or primary source of income was alimony or child-support payments. Creditors argued that such income was notoriously unreliable. So, these women sometimes elected to omit the source of this income when they applied for credit. Today, a woman does not have to reveal that any or all of her income comes from child support and/or alimony. But if she does, a creditor cannot automatically refuse her credit. The creditor can, however, ask for proof that these payments are made regularly: photocopies of an ex-husband's regular checks and a copy of the court order that states the ex-wife's right to this income will help convince a lender that the income is reliable.

If your marital status changes, a creditor cannot cancel the accounts you hold in your own name or make you reapply, unless there is some evidence that you no longer intend to pay your bills. However, if you and your husband had joint accounts and you are divorced or widowed, a creditor can ask you to reapply—if your husband's income was used as a factor in determining your credit worthiness originally.

A creditor cannot automatically reject your application just because you receive social security benefits, welfare, or some other form of public assistance. But you must meet the creditor's other requirements for credit worthiness, too. Creditors do have the right to inquire about such factors as the ages of your dependents.

Age and Credit

In the past, older people of both sexes sometimes found their credit cancelled or credit limit lowered. Sometimes a new widow was denied credit, despite her husband's good credit history. ECOA allows a widow to share her husband's credit record, but it also makes it easier for older people to maintain or begin credit arrangements. Now, a creditor cannot lower or cancel your credit just because you reach 62 or 65; reaching this age no longer means that you automatically become less credit worthy when the lender scores your application. A creditor must also count your retirement income as a factor.

A creditor does have the right to ask you certain questions related to your age: if your income is stable, and if it will drop or cease when you retire. But a creditor must consider this information and the rest of your credit history independently of your age; it cannot be a factor in making a decision to grant or withhold credit.

Using Credit Wisely

Credit is a convenience—but it almost always costs you money. Many people find that plastic money is *too* convenient; owning a credit card sometimes seems to be a license to spend. Too often, consumers charge up to their limit on two, three, or five cards. When the bills come in, they are startled to see how much they have charged and how much finance charges add to the total. Sometimes a consumer who has overextended herself finds that she must take out a loan to repay her immediate bills. The additional finance charges, she discovers, make the total cost of such a loan extraordinarily high, and they commit her to a long period of skimping. Yet she has little choice but to take the loan if she wishes to get out of her immediate financial bind.

A wise consumer—including many who have painfully worked their ways out of financial binds like that above—learns to use credit sparingly and carefully. She uses credit only for large purchases, paying cash for routine expenses. In this way, she does not end up paying high finance charges for groceries, gas, clothes, and incidentals. Some carry only one major credit card, as a convenience for identification, cashing checks, and emergencies. Any other cards are at home, in a locked desk drawer or a file, and they are used only for major purchases that have been well considered.

TRUTH IN LENDING ACT

If you decide to use credit, it is wise to comparison shop for the best deal. Two stores may offer the same merchandise at the same price, but one store may charge a much higher rate of interest, increasing the total cost. Further, you may find that one bank or store requires too high a monthly payment—it would be easier for you to pay a small amount monthly over a long period of time. On the other hand, if you can easily manage a relatively high monthly payment, you save yourself the additional interest. Federal Truth in Lending laws make comparing possible types of credit easier.

The Truth in Lending Act is the common name for the Federal Consumer Protection Act of 1969. According to the Truth in Lending Act, all creditors are required to explain exactly how much you will have to pay for using credit. This Federal law was designed to reduce consumers' confusion as they compare credit prices. The law requires all sellers and lenders to state the cost of credit clearly, and requires all sellers and lenders to use the same phrases and words to describe the terms of borrowing.

As you comparison shop, you should pay particular attention to two factors—the finance charge and the annual percentage rate. The finance charge is the amount of money you pay for the convenience of using credit to buy an item. That includes any interest, service charges, and miscellaneous fees. If you are getting a loan for a single item—a car, say—you can calculate its total cost by adding the purchase price to the finance charge.

Comparing the annual percentage rate of various creditors is a helpful way of comparison shopping. The annual percentage rate—also called the "interest rate"—is the amount you pay for credit in a year, expressed as a percentage. The annual percentage rate is a convenient way of comparing credit terms. If you are offered a loan at an interest rate of 7½ percent, for instance, but discover that as a college student you might borrow the same amount for 2½ percent, you will be wise to take the lower priced loan.

Creditors have an obligation, under the Truth in Lending Act, to itemize all their charges and clearly set forth the finance charge and annual percentage rate. Even with these figures, however, variables can be confusing. If you prefer low monthly payments, it may be to your advantage to deal with a creditor who allows small payments but charges a higher interest rate. You have a right to understand your credit agreements, and a prospective creditor has a legal obligation to explain any confusing items or terms. If the credit officer or loan officer cannot or will not explain the charges, you should not sign the loan application.

CREDIT REFUSAL, MISINFORMATION, AND MISTAKES

A prospective creditor must tell you whether your application has been approved within 30 days after you complete the application. If you are refused credit, or if your credit is cancelled, you have the right to know why, in writing. Be sure to require this information; there might be an error on your credit record, which you can correct. Or if your application was turned down because you have just moved into town, you can request the credit bureau in your old town to send your file. If you have been turned down because you have asked for more money than one bank thinks you can afford to repay, you can reapply for less money, or try another institution.

Not all creditors use the same system to judge credit worthiness. Some travel and entertainment credit cards, for instance, are very hard to acquire, while bank credit cards with similar privileges are relatively easy to get. If your loan or credit application is turned down, simply try another creditor.

If you feel that you have been discriminated against, however, you should tell the lender so. If a clear and satisfactory explanation is not forthcoming at this point, contact your lawyer.

Fair Credit Reporting Act

If you are told that your credit record contains derogatory information, ask for the name of the credit bureau that furnished the report. Contact that bureau and ask to see your credit history. Under the provisions of the Fair Credit Reporting Act, you have a right to see and understand your own credit record.

The Fair Credit Reporting Act of 1970 (FCRA) enables you to see a summary of your credit record and also helps you to correct any mistakes your record includes. This Federal law also states that you have the right to decide who may see your credit file. Prospective creditors will be given access, but private individuals have no right to examine your history. The law also guarantees that you can be informed when a bureau is asked for a report. It gives you the right to find out the results of this inquiry and the right to be told which prospective creditors have seen your history in the last six months.

In investigating your credit history, a credit bureau will often contact your employer, your previous creditors, your bank, and your landlord. Sometimes it will ask your neighbors for information. The bureau does not normally verify information from these sources, and it is possible that some of their facts are inadvertently wrong. You have the right, under FCRA, to ask for a summary of your credit history, and if you have trouble analyzing the technical information in your file, the law states that the credit bureau must give you free help in understanding it. The bureau can charge a fee for the summary, unless you are investigating a credit refusal that occurred within the last 30 days. To contact your credit bureau—there may be several in your area—ask your bank for the name of the bureau they use and find their address in the phone book.

If you find an apparent error, notify the credit bureau. They will conduct further investigations into the source of the information and will remove any records they find to be inaccurate. If you do not agree with their findings, you can write a short summary explaining your version of the matter. The credit bureau must give a copy of this statement to every firm that has previously asked to see your credit file, as well as to those that may ask to see it in the future.

The FCRA offers you other rights, too. Some negative information can be removed from your file after a time. If you have been involved in legal proceedings—for instance, if you were arrested or sued—you can ask that your record drop this fact after seven years. If you have been a bankrupt, your file can omit this information after 10 years.

Fair Credit Billing Act

With modern computerized systems of billing, errors sometimes can be stubborn. The Fair Credit Billing Act of 1976 enables you to question and correct billing errors without penalty to your credit history. There are several situations the law defines as "billing errors," which can be remedied under this law. The FCBA applies if:

- Your bill reflects purchases made by someone who is not authorized to use your card.
- Your bill includes items you did not buy.
- You have been charged for goods or services that either were not delivered on time or were refused at delivery.
- You question the charges or need more information than the bill provides.
- The bill includes an arithmetic error, misstates the original purchase price, or its date is not the same as the purchase date.
- The bill does not credit your account for payments you have made.
- The bill has not been mailed to a new address, providing that you told your creditor of your move at least 10 days before his or her billing period ended.

If you do have a billing problem, first contact the creditor by phone or in person. Gather together any relevant cancelled checks and bills. Photocopy the originals and, if you write to the creditor, send copies of these documents. Keep the originals on hand for your own files. A call or letter can straighten out most problems.

If this does not solve the problem, however, write the creditor. Under the law, you must write to the creditor within 60 days of the date the bill was mailed. In your letter, give your name and account number, and explain your reasons for believing your bill is in error. Within 30 days, the creditor must have acknowledged your letter; he or she has 90 days to resolve the dispute by correcting the error or explaining why the bill is deemed right as written.

While you wait for the creditor to reply, you must pay any undisputed parts of your bill. But the creditor cannot try to collect the disputed amount in the 90-day period or tell a credit bureau that you are delinquent, providing that you pay all undisputed charges.

If the creditor agrees that a mistake has been made, your account must be corrected without penalty. But if the creditor disagrees, you must be given a new bill, which will usually include the finance charges that have accumulated. At this point, the creditor may legally report your bill to a credit agency as overdue. If you do not pay, your bill can be given to a collection agency.

If you are still unsatisfied with your creditor's explanation, inform the creditor so in writing. Then contact your attorney if the problem is not corrected.

If, at this point, you have informed a creditor in writing that you still disagree with your bill, the creditor must give that information to your credit bureau. The bureau, then, must send you the names of any firms or people who have seen your credit history. The creditor has a legal obligation to tell all of these the final outcome of your dispute. You can, if you wish, write a short summary of your opinion of the dispute to be included in your file.

Unsolicited, Lost, or Stolen Credit Cards

In the past, firms sometimes mailed credit cards to people who had not requested them. This is now illegal under the Truth in Lending Act. However, if you already have an account with a firm, it can automatically send you an unsolicited card when your original card has expired.

Before the Truth in Lending Act, the cardholder was responsible for all debts incurred, even if the card had been lost, stolen, or misused. Today, the limit of the cardholder's liability is $50 per card, and in any case the law states that you are liable only if all these conditions have been met:

- The issuer must provide some means of identifying the authorized user: either by "signature, photograph, fingerprint on the card, or by electronic or mechanical confirmation."
- The issuer must have sent you a stamped envelope that you can use to report a stolen card.

- The issuer must have informed you that you have a potential liability of $50.
- You must have asked for the card or allowed another person to use it.

If your card or cards are lost or stolen, phone all the companies that issued the cards immediately. Your bank, the phone book, and old bills from the issuers can help you to determine where to call. As a safeguard, you should also immediately fill out and mail all issuers the self-addressed forms they originally sent with the cards. If there is any dispute about bills that are incurred on a stolen card, you should follow the procedures for billing problems outlined above.

chapter 16

Widowhood

problems of settling estates

The average American wife has a head start toward outliving her husband, since she is about three years younger than he. Then too, women tend to live approximately four years longer than men of the same age. This totals up to the fact that a wife can expect to outlive her husband by about seven years.

As greater numbers of married women work or pursue careers outside the home, they become increasingly knowledgeable about legal and financial affairs. Many of them automatically share the responsibility for handling finances with their husbands, and some wives assume this task entirely. Frequently, however, the husband handles all the family finances. When the husband dies, his widow often feels that she has not had the experience or education to begin coping with family finances. The problems raised by death and estate settlement are added to her burdens, and she usually faces these tasks when she is alone or in poor health.

To avoid such potential dangers, every married couple should anticipate and minimize the problems that may arise. Perhaps the most important step is to make certain that you know of all insurance, property rights, stocks and bonds, bank accounts, social security, pension and retirement income, and other assets that may be available to you. Discussing these matters with your husband can help guarantee that you will take advantage of all these assets if you need to when the time comes. Too often, wives assume that they will be able to identify and obtain assets or inheritance rights, but experience shows that widows frequently cheat themselves of benefits because they have not been told about some assets.

LISTING ASSETS

Few of us like to give much thought to the possibility of death. But a married woman may find it helpful to have a financial conference with her husband. Of course, some men will feel that this is an intrusion, but every wife should insist that she becomes knowledgeable about the basics of their financial status. In the interest of your security, it is a good idea to keep a written record of your assets and liabilities for future reference.

BANK ACCOUNTS

#1 Name on account; joint or individual ________________

Location of bank ________________

Passbook number and place where it is kept ________________

#2 Name on account; joint or individual ________________

Location of bank ________________

Passbook number and place where it is kept ________________

#3 Any Additional accounts

SAFE DEPOSIT BOXES

#1 Name of holder; joint or individual ______________________

May wife have access in event of husband's death? _______

Location of safe deposit box ____________________________

Where is access key retained? ___________________________

What does safe deposit box contain? (detailed inventory may be attached)

____

____

____

LIFE INSURANCE POLICIES

#1 Name of company ______________________________________

Face amount of policy ___________________________________

Where policy is kept ____________________________________

Beneficiary ____

#2 Name of company ______________________________________

Face amount of policy ___________________________________

Where policy is kept ____________________________________

Beneficiary ____

#3 Group life insurance policies at work, etc.

REAL ESTATE OWNED

#1 Property at ____

Type of ownership (joint, etc.) __________________________

Amount owed on mortgage or deed or trust ______________

#2 ____

(add additional property)

that she would properly provide for their children. With property valued at about $350,000, the wife can receive all of the estate tax free under existing Federal estate tax laws.

However, if the wife managed to hold on to her inheritance for the remainder of her life and did not remarry, the entire value of $350,000 would be subject to taxes under Federal estate laws, upon her death. About half of the $350,000 would be exempted, but the estate tax eventually paid by the heirs would be approximately $47,000.

After talking to his attorney, the husband learned that by leaving about half of his estate ($175,000) outright to his wife by will and leaving $175,000 as a trust fund, the husband could avoid Federal estate tax payments, both at the time of his death and on the subsequent death of his wife. The trust was set up so that the principal was invested and the income made payable to the wife. In addition, the trust principal could be available to the wife if she should ever be in need. Although there would be estate tax rates, exemptions, and deductions, the money in the trust would remain in a sort of taxation limbo until it was eventually passed on to the children. The effect of the trust, however, would be that all $350,000 of the husband's estate would be given to the children, free of Federal estate tax. This would eventually save the heirs $47,000.

In most instances, estate planning is a complicated study beyond the scope of this book. People with unusual assets or property may need the assistance of a tax expert and/or a tax attorney to plan the best course of action. How an individual's will is set up sometimes makes a considerable difference in the amount of estate taxes that must be paid, but only a practiced expert can be sure to set up a secure trust. Since both husband and wife may be interested in protecting the rights and assets of their children, both may want to become involved in estate planning for the future benefit of their heirs.

THE WILL

Every married woman should make sure that her husband has made a will, that she can locate the will, and that she is aware of its provisions. Many people think, wrongly, that they do not need a will, since they own a relatively small amount of property, or since they believe that property automatically passes to the spouse because of joint ownership. Neither of these common assumptions is necessarily true.

Experienced legal authorities also suggest that a married woman have her own will. The preparation of the document is a learning technique in itself, and a will allows her to insure that her own personal property will be distributed as she wishes. This may also help to avoid the bitter family fights that occur all too often when heirs argue about the distribution of an inheritance. A well-made will can spell out exactly who gets what.

With rare exceptions, a will should be drawn up by a lawyer, who will seldom charge much more for preparing the wife's will if it is made at the time one is drafted for the husband.

Advantages of Husband's Will

There are almost always legal advantages in leaving your property by will, but there are seldom any advantages in dying without making one. (The legal term for dying without a will is dying *intestate*.)

If you leave no will, the law of the state where you die specifies which of your heirs will receive your property and in what proportions. The state laws on descent and distribution (legally sometimes called *laws of devise and descent*) seldom correspond with the suppositions and desires of the person who dies without a will. And there are no uniform laws from state to state that insure who will get the deceased's property.

Approximately 75 percent of all adults interviewed in a survey covering several states were unable to identify correctly the specific relatives that property would pass to if they died without a will. Too often, widows of men who die intestate are shocked and distressed to find that the husband's property is not distributed as he had assumed it would be; their seemingly secure future vanishes.

In the majority of cases, the husband intends to provide some financial security to his widow and children if he dies. Most husbands believe that the wife will automatically receive whatever property can be passed on. In a number of states, this impression can be quite misleading. According to the law in some jurisdictions, the surviving wife is entitled to either one-third or one-half of the husband's property. In a few states, the wife's share is equal to that of each minor child. If the couple had seven children, the wife would receive only one-eighth of the estate.

There is usually a greater need for a will if a couple has minor children. Minors own the property that they inherit, but they are not permitted to exercise legal rights to handle the property (to sell, lease, rent, or whatever) until they become of legal age. If the minor inherits from a parent who leaves no will, a legal guardian must be appointed. This means additional costs for bonding the guardian, with charges and fees for court supervision and accounting. Of course, the wife would probably qualify as the court-appointed guardian of her minor children and would, therefore, have the authority to distribute their funds. But in most states a guardian needs court approval to spend the minor children's money for anything but the barest of necessities. In addition, the surviving wife-guardian would be supervised, and accountable to the court for each expenditure. A court order is usually necessary before a minor's money may be used to pay college expenses, for example. Besides, there is always a possibility that the supervising judge and the mother may disagree concerning what appears to be a reasonable request to spend money on the child. A widow who is involved in court matters that arise from guardianship loses valuable time and gains unnecessary stress. Then too, court costs that are an automatic part of such a procedure may eat heavily into the estate funds that the husband intended for the family. An outright bequest of the husband's money and property to the mother usually avoids the problems of guardianship that automatically arise in cases of intestancy. Obviously, neither a husband nor a wife should refuse to make a will, unless they are not concerned about how their funds are to be used.

Then too, in most instances, the heirs will usually be slower to receive their inheritances when there is no will. This delay, usually the result of crowded court calendars, often comes at a time when the heirs are in real need.

When a person dies without a will, an administrator or administratrix to settle the estate must be appointed by the court. (If a person who has a will dies, the court appoints the individual you name as an executor or executrix.) The person appointed to act as administrator or administratrix is legally required to put up a bond. In many states, this bond is at least 1½ percent of the estimated value of the estate. An even higher bond is required by the courts in some instances. The purpose of the bond is to make sure that the administrator or administratrix will not embezzle or steal some of the estate's assets.

Funds for the administrative bond are taken from the estate's assets. This, of course, is some of the money that may be needed by the deceased's wife and children. If a bond is necessary, it ties up those funds. In writing a will, the maker can specify that a bond of this kind can be waived for the executor or executrix. Usually, a lawyer will suggest that the will waives the bond, since the executor or executrix—often a surviving spouse, a reliable relative, or close friend—can be trusted not to steal from the estate. And in a large number of cases, the only heirs are the surviving spouse and the deceased's children. If the living spouse has been appointed executrix or executor, it is usually inappropriate to require that spouse to post bond to insure that the couple's minor children will not be cheated, but if there is no will this bond must be made.

Some additional costs and fees may be assessed if the estate settlement is made by an administrator or administratrix, rather than by an executor or executrix under the terms of a will. Probate court officials and lawyers sometimes point out that in a modest estate left without a will, the estate may shrink to one-third of the total original value.

If the deceased left no will, some of the real property (land, houses, real estate) may go to the minor children. The sale of this kind of property will be under the detailed supervision of the court. Since court approval must be obtained to sell any property of a minor, it often happens that a widow receives a good offer for the sale of such property, only to have the offer expire before court approval can be obtained. One of the advantages of writing a will is that this requirement for court supervision may be waived as one of the provisions in a will. The executor or executrix may then dispose of the property by sale when the best offer is obtained. Under a so-called *independent* or *nonintervention* will, which your attorney can write, the executrix or executor is independent of court supervision. If your will authorizes your executrix or executor to settle the estate without putting up a bond, the executrix or executor will still be legally liable for fraud or for seriously mishandling the assets of the estate.

Who Can Make a Will?

There are age requirements in all states for anyone wanting to make a will. Usually, the maker must be 21 years of age, but some states permit the making of a will at 18, or even as early as 14 under some circumstances. Any local attorney can advise you about this.

SERVING AS EXECUTRIX

Frequently, a husband's will designates his wife to serve as executrix of his estate. He reasons that his wife will inherit much of his property and knows that no one will be more interested in the property than she will. In other situations, it is usual to designate an adult daughter or son, or a professional executor or executrix, such as an attorney. Serving as executrix is usually well within the abilities of any adult.

The settlement of an estate is under the jurisdiction of the state court usually referred to as the *probate court*. In most states, the probate court is legally called a *trial court of general jurisdiction*. In a few states, it may be known as the *orphan's court*, *surrogate court*, or *court of ordinary*. If you are named executrix of a will, you can find the court to contact under one of these names in the book, among the county offices. The county clerk, your bank, or your lawyer can also tell you where this court is located. In a few of the less populous states, handling of probate (wills and trusts) is only part of the duties of a regular trial court of general jurisdiction.

The first job for the executrix is to appear before this probate court with the will. The county clerk, or the clerk of the court, can tell you where and when to appear. The court then sets up procedures to examine the will, so that the judge can be satisfied that it is the genuine will of the deceased. It may be necessary to call in one or more people who witnessed the will, but this proof is seldom in dispute. The judge orders the court clerk to prepare a document for the judge's signature, called *letters of administration* or *letters testamentary*. This document is simply legal authority for the executrix to settle the estate. As a practical matter, a copy of the letters of administration should accompany almost every request for action that the executrix sends out.

At the start of the estate settlement, the executrix should ask the clerk of the probate court for a printed statement of her powers and authority as executrix. Unless the will specifically exempts the executrix from this requirement, she will have to post a bond to guarantee that estate assets are not mishandled or stolen.

Basically, it is the job of the executrix to draw up a list of the deceased's assets, collect and preserve them, pay outstanding debts and all taxes due, and then distribute the property or money that is left. This must all be done to the approval of the court.

First, however, the executrix should examine the will to determine whether it gives her powers to conduct business, borrow money, settle claims, and so on, beyond the powers given by state law. She can rely on the advice of the county clerk in interpreting her powers. Ideally, for ease of settlement, the will should be drawn up to contain a provision stating that the executrix has authority to sell property, to assign values at the time of sale without a property appraisal, and to conduct any type of business or negotiate debts. Unless these powers are given by the will, the executrix must wait for court approval for sales of property and cannot borrow on the estate assets.

The executrix is required to prepare an inventory of the estate's assets. This can best be done by going through all old checks, personal papers, bank safe deposit boxes, brokerage accounts, and other financial records. Sometimes it is necessary to obtain property appraisals from experts in the real estate field. Usually the clerk of the probate court can direct the executrix concerning the necessary techniques for appraisal of asset worth.

The executrix is required to pay all the deceased's debts out of the estate. So that there is no doubt, most states require the executrix to advertise to locate creditors, giving them about six months in which to file claims. The estate may not be settled before this statutory time has expired.

In many instances, taxes will not be due to either the Federal or state tax authorities unless the estate is of considerable worth. Tax reports must be filed, however, before real estate can be transferred and before the estate can be closed. The preparation of these tax returns usually requires the help of specially trained tax experts. One reason that estates close so slowly is that tax authorities must have time to review these returns.

Distribution of assets can cause problems. If the executrix cannot persuade the heirs to hold property jointly, she must sell the property and divide the proceeds among the heirs who are entitled to share. Frequently, stocks and title to real estate may be transferred directly to heirs, and the clerk of the court can usually be of help here. Real estate transfers, however, may require the services of an attorney. Costs of necessary specialists such as tax preparers and lawyers are paid by the estate, of course, rather than by the executrix. In most states, the executrix is paid fees and a specified percentage of the estate for her duties.

chapter 17

Benefits

social security, pensions, retirement

SOCIAL SECURITY

Social security is the Federal government's pension program. If, during all or part of your adult life, you and/or your husband worked and contributed to social security, chances are good that you and your dependents have a right to receive payments when you reach age 62. (If you are eligible and choose to begin receiving payments at 62, your checks will be smaller than if you wait until age 65.)

Determining if you are eligible for social security and, if so, the size of your payments can become a complex matter. A call or a visit to your local social security office will help to explain your specific rights. This chapter outlines some common situations.

Household Workers

All women who are employed full time or part time should make sure that their employers regularly contribute part of their paychecks to the

Social Security Administration. Usually, employers do this automatically, but those who employ household workers—cooks, maids, gardeners, babysitters, chauffeurs, and so on—often do not make this contribution. If you are a household worker and earn at least $50 in a three-month period (calendar quarter), you are eligible for some social security benefits—but only if you have a social security card, and if you make sure your employer reports your income to the government.

All Employed Women

Women workers, whether or not they have interrupted their careers, are normally eligible for social security payments. A woman who works part time or who has worked for only part of her adult life will not, of course, receive as much compensation as a woman who has worked throughout her life.

If you are married, you can receive payment on the basis of your husband's records or on your own. (Wives receive 50 percent of their husband's checks at age 65, but if you have been employed all your life, your own benefit will probably be higher than this.) Even if your husband decides to continue working past age 65, you can receive benefits starting at age 62 if you retire.

If you interrupted your career for a period of years, your social security office can help you to determine if you can receive payments when you are old enough. Women who gave up paid work when they were married often find that they will receive more as a wife (if the husband is eligible for social security) than they would on the basis of their own work records. If this is the case, your rights are explained later in this section.

If your benefit is considerably higher than that your husband would receive based on his own earnings, he may want to take the spouse's benefit, which is based on your work record rather than on his own. The social security office can tell you which payment would be higher, and arrange for him to receive the better one.

If your husband takes the spouse's benefit and is dependent on your social security records for his checks, the checks will continue if you die, but they will cease if he remarries.

If you return to employment after beginning to receive social security checks, you must report this. Too much monthly income or too many working hours may reduce or end your checks.

Disability or Death

If, at any age, you have a disability that is expected to last at least one year, you and your husband or children may be able to receive compensation. Inform the social security office of your situation; checks will not be sent until you have been disabled for five months. Your unmarried children (including adoptees and stepchildren) will receive checks if they are under age 18 (or if they are under 22, providing they are full-time students). If you die, your unmarried children will receive monthly checks until they become too old for eligibility.

If you are disabled, your husband may be able to receive checks on the basis of your record if he is 62 or older. He, too, will receive payments monthly if you die, unless he remarries before the age of 60.

Social security makes a small lump-sum death payment to survivors. It is intended to help defray funeral arrangements.

Working in the Home

If you chose to work in your home or if the social security benefits you earned in the course of your employment are substantially less than your husband's, you can often take advantage of his social security record, whether you are now married, divorced, or widowed. If you have earned much less than your husband during your working years, your social security check may be larger if you opt to take a wife's benefit (50 percent of the husband's check) rather than the benefit your own earnings would bring. If you are employed, however, you may not be eligible for benefits until you quit your job.

Women Currently Married

You are also eligible for social security at age 62 if your husband receives social security because he is disabled or has retired. (Once again, your checks will be larger if you wait until you are 65 to claim them.) If you have an unmarried child of 18 or younger at home, or a disabled child of any age, you are entitled to payments when your husband retires or becomes disabled, no matter what your age is.

Widows

If you take the spouse's benefit based on your husband's lifelong contributions to social security, your checks will continue as long as you live, even if your husband dies and you remarry. If your husband is receiving social security checks and he dies, you should inform the social security office and return any checks that come for him after his death. You will receive a small payment to help with funeral expenses.

You are eligible for a widow's benefit automatically, no matter how old you are, if you have a dependent child under 18 or your unmarried child is a full-time student under 22. Once your children go beyond the allowed ages, however, your status may change. Social security also gives benefits to all widows who care for disabled children, no matter what age the widow or child is.

If you are childless, or if your children are independent, you must be 60 years old to receive a widow's pension, unless you are disabled. In that case, your benefits can begin at age 50.

If you remarry after age 59, your benefits will continue. Check with the social security office, however, to determine which would be larger—your benefit as a widow or your benefit as your new husband's wife. You will be given the larger payment.

If you remarry before you are 60, your benefits will cease, but if the new marriage ends, you may be eligible for a widow's pension on the basis of your first husband's contribution to social security. Check with the office.

Divorced Women

With few exceptions, the wife's benefits stop if you and your husband are divorced after benefits begin. Legally, you must report a divorce to your local social security office. There are, however, exceptions. A divorced woman may qualify for benefits if she fits one of these descriptions:

- She was married at least ten years, is at least 62 years old, and has not remarried.
- She is disabled, was married at least ten years, and is at least 50.
- She has minor children who are eligible for benefits on the basis of her ex-husband's record.

If you receive benefits on the basis of your ex-husband's social security contributions, these benefits will stop when you remarry. (Here again, you must report to social security.) You may, however, qualify for payments as your new husband's wife. And, as stated earlier, if your new marriage ends, you may still be eligible to reapply and receive checks on the basis of your earlier husband's social security contributions. Discuss this possibility with a representative of your local office.

If you are a divorced woman with a minor child or children, you usually can be allotted a mother's benefit if your ex-husband dies, provided that he was eligible for social security.

Children's Benefits

If you have dependent children and you receive social security, those children have a right to benefits, too. This applies to stepchildren and adopted children also. A child is eligible if he or she is unmarried and is either under 18, between 18 and 22 and a full-time student, or disabled, if the child was disabled before the age of 22. If a child who receives benefits becomes ineligible or dies, you must inform the social security office.

Name Changes

Whether or not you work and make social security contributions, if you change your name, you should go to your social security office and fill out a *Request for Change in Social Security Records*. Also, you will need to apply for a new card in your new name. Otherwise, your records are likely to become confused, and you may lose any benefits you accumulated as a worker or a wife under your first name.

Checks

Normally, social security checks are timed to arrive in your mailbox on the third or fourth of every month. Many people, however, prefer their checks to be mailed directly from the Social Security Administration to their banks. This system is called *direct deposit*, and it eliminates worries about lost or stolen checks.

If you do not have a checking or savings account, you can start one and arrange for your social security checks to be deposited directly. (You may want to ask the bank or savings and loan if they have any special services for older people, such as free checking accounts.) At the bank, ask for Form SF-1199; bank personnel will help you to fill in the information on the form. About 90 days after the Social Security Administration receives the form from your bank, your checks will begin to be mailed directly to the bank. Usually, the bank will send a receipt confirming that your check has been credited to your account.

If you lose a check or if it is stolen, contact your local social security office as soon as possible. They will replace the check, but paperwork will delay your new check—it may not come for a while.

Disagreeing on Benefits

If you feel that social security rules discriminate against you or that a mistake has been made in evaluating your situation, inform your social security office. They will discuss the matter with you. If you still feel that the decision is wrong, you can carry the matter further, to the Office of Hearings and Appeals. You will be granted a hearing in front of a judge. From there, if you are still not convinced, your case can be reviewed by an appeals court, and from there can go to federal court. At any point in this procedure, you can be represented by an attorney, but you must pay the attorney's fees. For more information, ask for the *Social Security and Your Right to Representation* pamphlet in your local social security office.

PENSION AND RETIREMENT FUNDS

Employee Retirement Income Security Act of 1974

Not long ago, a woman interested in investigating her pension rights, contributions, and benefits was usually discouraged by the forbidding legal language of most pension plans. Since the passage of the Employee Retirement Income Security Act of 1974 (ERISA), however, understanding your pension plan is much easier. This federal law requires every participant in a pension plan to receive a clear, comprehensible summary of the plan. This summary will explain how benefits will be paid. It will give information as to whether the worker's surviving spouse may be entitled to any benefits. The summary also describes your right to examine all the documents relating to the plan.

If you are fired, quit, or become permanently disabled and you are entitled to future benefits, your employer (or pension plan's administrator) is legally obligated to provide you with a statement as to your amount of future benefits. Otherwise, you have a right to request this information once a year, and it must come to you within 30 days. Every year, your employer must furnish you with a summary of the plan's annual report.

A pension plan establishes a fund that will provide you with periodic payments when you retire from your job. The money in your pension fund comes either from company funds, or from company funds and from your paycheck. So, the pension you receive when you retire is, really, money that your employer has kept and invested for you.

Before ERISA became law, pension plans often required an employee to work at one job until retirement age in order to receive benefits. In the past, employees who left a firm after working for only a few years often lost any right to future benefits; sometimes an employee would be fired shortly before retirement and would, therefore, lose all benefits. Employers reasoned, perhaps unfairly, that an employee who left a job for whatever reason lost the right to retirement benefits. But the money in the pension fund, after all, was really part of the person's wages, either actual or deferred; the employer had no real right to keep the money.

ERISA partially corrects this situation. In general, the employer can require no more than 15 years' service before you have a right to all of your benefits. Often only 10 years are required. If you work less, you might have a right to some benefits, depending on the plan.

How Contributions Are Determined

There are two ways of funding pension plans. In some plans, you must make contributions from your paycheck. Other plans do not require you to do this; the employer makes contributions from company earnings.

If you must contribute, the amount of your salary that is paid into a pension plan depends on a variety of factors: your age, sex, salary, estimated year of retirement, and so on. Actuaries—the mathematicians who calculate pension costs and insurance rates—try to determine pension contributions to be as fair as possible. So, a worker who works part time and earns a small salary and makes smaller contributions to a company pension fund will end up with small retirement benefits. The executives, however, will contribute more to the fund and will receive larger payments when they retire.

Responsible actuaries try to insure that no one group of workers in a firm subsidizes other groups of workers. The contributions you make should correspond to the benefit you will eventually receive. For example, if you begin working at age 40, you should expect to make higher contributions than a worker who began at age 20, if you expect to receive the same retirement benefits.

Equal Contributions for Men and Women?

Sometimes employers require women and men who work at the same job for the same salary to contribute different amounts to a company pension fund. Actuaries figure that women as a group live longer than men and that, therefore, women should give more to the company pension fund; the reasoning here is that women will normally be drawing retirement funds for more years than men who retire at the same age.

Understandably enough, some women feel that this is unfair, and the legal status of this practice is currently unclear. Women who object to this practice feel that it discriminates against them. They also argue that no individual woman knows how long she will live. If she dies soon after retirement, her many years of larger pension payments deprive her of income during her life.

There is another side of the argument, however. Premiums for insurance policies and contributions for pension plans are determined in a similar manner. In setting insurance rates, actuaries consider that the rates for women are lower than those for men. Therefore, if pension plans discriminate against women, then it follows that insurance discriminates against men. The question of whether there is any discrimination here is an open one. If the courts finally conclude that discrimination does exist, we may expect men to raise the issue of whether insurance discriminates against them.

chapter 18

Parent-Child Responsibilities

Anyone who has the custody or guardianship of a child has certain rights and obligations, but some of these rights and obligations vary, depending on whether the child is legitimate. The first section of this chapter is addressed to anyone who has custody of a child. The second section, on "legitimate children," describes common legal situations and problems. The third section, on "illegitimate children," discusses the specific legal questions that arise when a child's parents are not married.

RIGHTS AND OBLIGATIONS

Usually, a child's legal parents are the woman and man who conceived the child—the child's natural parents—but the law allows certain variances from this rule. If the natural parents gave the child up for adoption, the adoptive parents are the parents in the eyes of the law, and the natural mother and father have no more parental rights and duties. If a child is born to a married woman as a result of artificial insemination from a donor other than her husband, the husband can be made the legal parent of the child (see later in this chapter under Illegitimate Children).

An orphan is often given a guardian by the courts, or by the terms of the parents' wills. There are three types of guardians, and they have different duties. (This subject is covered in more detail in Chapter 16.)

Rights of Children

In the eyes of the law, a child is a minor—someone who has not yet reached the age of majority. This age varies from state to state, but is usually either 18 or 21. A minor may not vote, and each state has its own laws regulating whether a minor may drive, purchase alcohol, be sentenced in court, or work.

A minor may make a contract, but the other party cannot force a minor to fulfill the bargain since, when the child reaches majority, he or she can disavow any contracts made before coming of age. In actual practice, this legal principle makes it unlikely that a firm or individual would enter into a contract with a minor.

Minors are usually responsible for the debts they incur themselves. However, some courts may rule that the parents are liable for the child's debts, since children have a right to necessities and proper care from their parents. ("Necessities" may be defined differently by different courts.)

A minor does not have the right to sue. However, a minor who is involved in a lawsuit can be represented by the parents, by a guardian, or by a court-appointed *guardian ad litem*, who can sue on the child's behalf. The guardian ad litem defends the child's rights in all civil lawsuits.

A child whose parent or parents have been killed or disabled can sue the person or people responsible for the wrong. If the child is an orphan, the guardian ad litem will handle the case in the child's name, and can demand damages.

Children have the right to be supported by their parents or guardians, to the extent these adults are able to support them. Naturally, the obligation to support usually ceases when the child reaches majority. The courts demand "reasonable" support, but have never specified exactly what "reasonable" standards or support and care are. A judge will make an individual decision, depending on the parent's financial standing.

The legal system, of course, distinguishes between parents who are unwilling to support their children and those who are unable to; children cannot be taken from home simply because the parents are poor or on welfare. But if any parent is unable or unwilling to support a child, the courts have the right to take the child away for the child's own good. This removal may be temporary or permanent, depending on circumstances, but parents who want their children returned to them would be wise to obtain the aid of a lawyer.

If a child's parent or guardian is unsuitable on account of cruelty, insanity, or for some other reason, the courts—again acting for the child's good—can step in, placing the child in a foster home. In practice, this happens rarely, but a parent whose child has been taken should consult an attorney for advice if she wishes to get the child back.

Normally, the parent's duty to support applies only to minor children, but there are some exceptions. Children who are disabled, either mentally or physically, may need permanent support.

If a child inherits money or property, the parents may not appropriate it, or use it in any way, without the court's permission. Normally, the property or money comes under the child's own management at majority; until that time, the property is overseen by a trustee named in the will. Even if the trustee is the child's own parent, however, the parent cannot sell property or use any money without the court's permission. The inheritance must be turned over intact at the child's majority. However, if some of these funds are absolutely necessary to support the child, the trustee can apply to the court that handled the will, asking for support money. For more information on guardianship, trusteeship, and inheritance law, see Chapter 16.

Occasionally, a minor child who supports him- or herself is named an "emancipated minor" by the courts. This happens in rare instances, when a child appears to have more resources of support and care than the parents have to offer—when, for instance, a child who has not received sufficient support from parents gets a job and responsibility supports him- or herself in his or her own apartment.

Rights and Obligations of Parents

Generally speaking, parents have certain rights, but in the eyes of the law, those rights can be withdrawn if the parent's duties and responsibilities toward the child are not fulfilled. Parents have the duty of providing adequate care and support for their children, although, as we have said, specific standards of care have never been set up by any court. Since the standards are as much social as legal, "adequate care" may be defined very differently, according to different parents' incomes, stations, and abilities. A very wealthy parent may be ordered to provide college money for a child, whereas no judge would expect a parent who receives welfare to fulfill such a court order.

Parents have the right to discipline children using "reasonable force," but they must not cause serious harm. In all cases involving children, the courts tend to make the child's good their principle interest. If parents fail in their duties—if they are cruel, will not give adequate support, desert their children, and so on—courts will usually deal harshly with the parents, punishing them and, in extreme cases, taking the children from them.

The courts have given agencies in charge of child welfare broad powers to investigate reports of child neglect and child abuse. Parents who are unable to support or care for their children should turn to public welfare agencies, or to institutions that provide care to orphans and deserted children.

If you know of or suspect a case of child abuse, you should contact the local police. In some areas, child abuse hotlines provide help to families with the problem; an operator can tell you if such a line exists in your area.

Parents' Right to Protect Children

You have the right to protect your children if they are threatened by injury or attack. You may use as much force as is necessary to repel the attack, but no more. So, if you see someone about to slap your child, you could rush in to separate them, or—if it was really necessary to prevent your child from being hurt—you could strike the attacker; but in this case, you could not shoot or cause unnecessary harm.

You may not revenge yourself upon someone who attacks or injures your child, whether or not you are present when the incident takes place. If you see a supermarket clerk strike your daughter because the clerk believes he saw her steal cookies, you do not have the right to attack the clerk, even if you know he was mistaken. You may, of course, prevent him from striking your child, using reasonable force. If the situation merits it, you should report the matter to the police, rather than try to punish the attacker. If your child is harmed, you do not have the right to punish the person who is responsible, and you may be in serious trouble if you do take the law in your own hands. You do, however, have the right to sue someone who hurts your child.

Parent Liability for Damages Created by Child

In most situations, parents are not liable for the damages or harm their children have created. However, there are exceptions. Every state in the United States will hold a parent responsibile for the damage the child creates if the parent is aware that the child is doing wrong and does not step in. For example, if you know that your daughter habitually fights with smaller children, you will be liable for any injuries she causes if you do not try to stop the bullying. Or if you know that your son spray-paints graffiti on others' property, and you do not break him of the habit, you will be liable if he decorates a neighbor's house.

You are also liable if your child causes harm while acting as your agent—whether or not the child acts maliciously. Usually, this situation arises when the child is doing errands. But occasionally a misguided parent gets a child to do some wrong to a neighbor, or revenge some supposed wrong, under the mistaken impression that neither the parent nor the child can be punished. The courts naturally disapprove of such tactics and will hold the parent responsible, requiring payment for any damages incurred.

You are also liable if you give your child a dangerous weapon or tool, or if you negligently allow a child access to such potentially harmful implements. For example, if you give your child a bow and arrow and he shoots someone, you are liable. You are also liable if your child finds your unlocked gun and, while playing with it, hurts someone. You may also be liable if, for example, you leave your power tools where children can get at them and your child hurts another child because of your negligence.

Parent Liability for Child's Car Accidents

You may be legally responsible if your child causes an auto accident while doing a chore for you (acting as your agent). State laws concerning negligence for liability vary so much that in many instances only a local attorney can tell you whether you are responsible.

Right to Sue on Child's Death or Injury

A parent or a guardian ad litem can bring a suit on a child's behalf if the child is injured in an accident or is hurt by some malicious person. If a child is injured or killed, parents may also sue on their own behalf to recover damages.

EDUCATION

Parents have an obligation to educate their children, either in private or public schools. Most educators and courts agree that home schooling is not adequate for children in the modern world, since it does not prepare the child for the social problems and adjustments necessary in daily life.

As a result of legislation in the 1970s, schools have an obligation to accept children with physical handicaps and learning disabilities into ordinary classrooms. In the past, these children often received no education, were educated at home, or were sequestered in special classrooms. Now, however, they have the right to be educated along with other children in local schools.

Laws about school attendance vary from state to state, and your local school board can give you information about local regulations. The minimum and maximum ages for school attendance varies by state. Schools have a right to demand that students be vaccinated and clean. Parents, of course, have the right to send their children to private schools, providing that these schools meet state standards.

It is not enough, however, to make sure that your children are enrolled in a school; parents have a duty to make sure that their children attend school regularly. If your child is habitually truant, you—or the school authorities—may ask a juvenile court to look into the matter. The court may, however, place the child in a reformatory if you are unable to control your offspring.

Schools in some districts have begun busing programs, attempting to bring schools into racial balance. Often, groups of parents who object to busing have found their objection struck down by the courts. In such cases, parents sometimes express their feelings by keeping their children home from school. The state, however, regards this as truancy and eventually may decide to enforce the law.

School's Right to Discipline Children

The rights of principals and teachers to discipline children and set rules of conduct vary from state to state, but, in general, courts agree that their rules of conduct and punishment must be reasonable. The punishments that may be administered are set by the school district and the state. In some states, a principal or teacher does not have the right to use corporal punishment at all. Here, detention, suspension of privileges, suspension, and expulsion are the standard practices. When corporal punishment is allowed, it too must be "reasonable"—gauged to the child's age, strength, and sex.

If you feel that your child has been punished unfairly or harshly, you have a right to sue either or both the school board and the individual teacher who struck your child. However, parents very rarely win this kind of case, since the courts begin by assuming the school's authorities acted properly. It is up to you and your attorney to prove otherwise. Normally, it is far better to discuss the matter with school authorities, even if the discipline seemed excessive.

Generally speaking, a school board or an individual teacher is not liable if your child is accidentally injured or killed while at school. If, however, the school or teacher was clearly negligent, a suit may be brought. For instance, if a child defies a school crossing guard, enters a crosswalk, and is hit by a car, the school is not liable. If, however, the crossing guard was an alcoholic who negligently let the child enter the crosswalk, the school might be liable.

SOCIAL AND SEXUAL LIVES OF CHILDREN

Parents have the right to decide when their minor children may date and who may come to visit them at their house. Practically, however, there is no way of enforcing this right, unless the parents wish the juvenile courts to take over. In this case, they can have the child charged with delinquency and taken from their care. Obviously, this is a fairly desperate solution. Most authorities would suggest that family counseling might be wiser and, in the long run, better for all concerned.

Again, courts are unlikely to take up time dealing with children who are sexually active. (In most states, sexual intercourse between two people who are not married to each other is a crime.) If a daughter is younger than the age of consent, however, the male can be charged with statutory rape (see Chapter 7).

If your daughter becomes pregnant, the father cannot be forced to marry her. However, if he admits responsibility—or if a paternity suit proves that he is responsible—he is liable for your daughter's pregnancy-related medical expenses and for child support until the child reaches majority.

Married Minor Children

Laws that outline the rights of married minor children and the obligations of their parents vary from state to state. In all cases, however, a minor child who intends to marry must have his or her parents' consent. Some states compel parents of married minors to continue support; others free them of this responsibility. A lawyer can describe the situation in your state. Marriage, incidentally, does not automatically give the rights of adulthood to a minor.

Child Employment

In the eighteenth and nineteenth centuries, the mills and factories of the Industrial Revolution needed cheap labor. Often, children as young as five or six were hired to do tedious, dangerous work, for 12 hours a day or more. Parents who desperately needed money to support their families sometimes had to send their children to work; orphans had little choice. Eventually, people who realized that children were being abused and killed by overwork and poor conditions called for lawmakers to limit child employment.

Today, child labor laws are stringent. They differ from state to state, but every state has set a minimum age for children who work, and states carefully oversee the working hours and schooling of children who hold jobs.

Most states give parents the right to claim all of a child's earnings. In practice, of course, many parents allow their children to keep what they earn.

Aid to Families with Dependent Children (AFDC)

AFDC is a federal program designed to assist children who have one parent who is disabled, who has deserted the family, or who has died. Children who qualify can receive small payments. The program is administered through welfare offices.

LEGITIMATE CHILDREN

A legitimate child is one born to a married woman. The child of a married couple is legally presumed to have been fathered by the woman's husband—whether or not that is in fact true. Recently, however, children born as a result of artificial insemination have in some circumstances made the issue of legitimacy unclear. If the sperm used is the husband's there is no problem, but if a donor provided it, the couple would be wise to visit a lawyer. The husband ought to sign a consent form that commits him to all the responsibilities and obligations of fatherhood—even if he later changes his mind. Otherwise, the legal situation may be very unclear. If the husband has acknowledged the child as his own, but then flees or refuses to support the child, courts will uphold the validity of the husband's original consent and will compel him to furnish support. The consent form also guarantees that the child can inherit from the husband.

Even now, the husband has the right to determine the surname of his children. The name he decides on does not necessarily have to be his own surname.

Parents have an obligation to support children, but the burden of supporting legitimate children has traditionally fallen most heavily on the father. Even if a marriage ends and the father leaves, he still must support his children (see Chapter 9). If the father dies, or if he cannot adequately support the children, the mother must do so.

Inheritance Rights

To guarantee that your money is distributed as you wish it to be, you should write a will. Otherwise, your money and property will be distributed according to state laws, which often do not correspond to the deceased's wishes (see Chapter 16).

Children's rights to inherit money from their parents vary from state to state. Usually, an adopted child has the same rights as a natural child. A lawyer who helps you to make your will can tell you if you need to specify that your adopted and natural children should be treated identically for inheritance purposes. A posthumous child—a child born after a parent dies—has the same inheritance rights as children born when both parents are alive.

Stepparents

If you have custody of your children and receive support from your ex-husband, and you decide to remarry, your new husband does not have any obligation to support your children. Your ex-husband must still send support payments. The same thing is true if your ex-husband has custody; if he remarries, you must still send any child support payments that are due.

It follows, then, that a stepparent does not have any legal obligation to support his or her stepchildren—unless the stepparent wants to adopt them. In this situation, the parent who does not have custody must give consent. When the adoption is final, the new parent takes on all parental rights and responsibilities, and the natural parent has no more legal interest in the children.

ILLEGITIMATE CHILDREN

An illegitimate child is one whose mother and father are not married to each other. However, the law presumes every child born to a married mother is legitimate, until there is proof to the contrary.

Children who are born illegitimate may suffer from a variety of legal and social disadvantages, through no fault of their own. In some circumstances, a child can be legitimated. Laws vary from state to state. Arizona and North Dakota, and Puerto Rico do not recognize any children as illegitimate unless the father is unknown. In most other states, you can make your child legitimate by marrying the father, either before or after the child is born. In a few states, the child's parents must marry, and the father must admit paternity, for the child to be "legitimate." An attorney can tell you the process your state follows.

Rights Which May Be Lost If a Child Is Illegitimate

Illegitimate children may not, in most states, claim their fathers' names. Usually, they cannot claim any inheritance from their fathers. (In Louisiana, a child may not even be able to inherit from the mother.) When a child is made legitimate, all mention of illegitimacy can be deleted from the birth certificate. In most states, a child who has been legitimated still has no right to inherit from the father's relations, and sometimes may not be able to inherit from the mother's family either.

Generally speaking, if you wish your illegitimate child to inherit from you, you should mention the child by name in your will and state what you wish the child to receive.

Support

An illegitimate child has the right to support from both parents, and under normal circumstances the law says that the mother must provide support only if the father cannot or will not. In fact, however, getting the father to provide support is not always easy. He may refuse, deny he is the father, or flee. If, at any point, the father signed an agreement to support the child, the courts can make him give that support. Otherwise, it may be necessary to hire an attorney and begin a paternity suit. If the suit is successful, the father must support the child's needs, but the child's support will not necessarily be proportionate to the father's income. That is, even if the father is extremely well off, his illegitimate child may not be able to expect a proportionately large support payment. The payment may only cover necessities.

Child's Name

An illegitimate child does not automatically have a right to the father's name. In this case, the mother has the right to decide the child's surname.

Custody

Until recently, the law automatically gave custody of an illegitimate child to the mother. This principle has been challenged successfully, however. Fathers have had mothers declared unfit and have been given custody of their children. But when a mother gives up her illegitimate child for adoption, the father does not normally have a right to demand that he be given custody of the child. He can, however, demand a hearing that may help him to win custody.

Further Rights

Minor illegitimate children have a right to social security benefits if either parent receives benefits. But if the father does not acknowledge his children, the children, their mother, or their guardian may have to institute a paternity suit to secure these payments.

chapter 19

Legal Help

getting it when you need it

Most of us can get through our day-to-day lives without detailed knowledge of the law and without the help of a lawyer. But there are times when advice and assistance may be critical. It is simply foolhardy not to obtain aid when you could needlessly lose your property, your rights, or your freedom. Of course, a simple matter like a traffic ticket may be handled by almost anyone. It is always wise, however, to consult an attorney when you are involved in a divorce, accused of a crime, faced with a lawsuit, or when you buy or sell property. But there are innumerable situations between these two extremes where help may also be advisable. In many of these situations, you can profit by an attorney's training, experience, and knowledge of the law.

Naturally, the lawyer you hire may not always win. But the attorney will be able to present your side of any dispute in its most favorable light.

DO-IT-YOURSELF LEGAL HELP

Recently, there has been a rash of books that promise to help resolve legal problems without hiring an attorney. There are, of course, instances when these publications may help. But all too often, people who do not have a lawyer's training do not recognize the problems and complications that may arise. If there is any doubt in your mind, you would be wise to consult a professional.

Cost-Free Sources

Sometimes you may be able to obtain free legal advice through national women's organizations or a variety of administrative and investigative agencies and boards at the Federal, state, and local levels. Sometimes the state Attorney General's office or Department of Consumer Affairs can offer free advice and assistance. In other situations—for example, if you need to interpret a city code, help can be obtained from the office of the City Attorney or Borough Attorney.

Other Specialists

Depending on the nature of your problem, you may find help from nonlegal sources. An accountant, tax specialist, realtor, actuary, engineer, real estate broker, or licensed architect may sometimes be in a better position to help you than an attorney is.

HIRING A LAWYER

Anyone accused of a serious crime is entitled to an attorney. You may hire your own, if you can afford to; if you cannot afford to pay an attorney, the state or federal government must furnish you one, free. Often this attorney will be from the public defender's office. If you request a free attorney when you, in fact, have the money or property that could be used to pay for your own attorney, however, you may be charged with the additional crime of perjury.

If the lawsuit or legal situation you are involved in does not involve a crime, it is a civil law problem. The government does not provide free lawyers for civil actions, so in most cases you must either hire an attorney or obtain free legal help.

Going about finding and hiring an attorney can seem confusing. There is no guaranteed way to find a good, reasonable one. Usually, people find attorneys through word of mouth, but in a city of any size you can find the number of the local bar association in the telephone directory. The association can usually help by recommending someone near you or someone who specializes in your particular kind of legal problem. Your bank or accountant can also be helpful in suggesting an attorney.

If you need to hire an attorney who will work in a distant city, you should ask your local bar association or a large local law firm if they will permit you to use the *Martindale and Hubbel Law Directory*. This is an encyclopedia that contains information about attorneys in all locations. Many large city libraries also have this directory.

Attorneys' Fees

You should not hesitate to call an attorney and discuss fees for a consultation. The lawyer will not charge for the conversation.

About half the people who visit an attorney have their problems resolved in a single visit. If more work is needed, you can make an arrangement to pay an hourly fee for the attorney's time. But if you call, most lawyers will be able to tell you what the fee for a specific procedure—a simple will, an adoption, a divorce—will be. If the problem takes up more of the attorney's time than is originally expected, the attorney's fees may go up.

Sometimes, especially if you sue for negligence or personal injury, an attorney will agree to work on a contingency basis. Rather than receiving a flat fee, the lawyer will receive a percentage of any money awarded to the client, if the case if successful. An attorney who accepts work on a contingency basis usually does so because the client does not have the resources to pay a bill and because the attorney feels that she or he has a good chance of winning the case. In effect, a lawyer who agrees to work for a contingency is gambling on his or her ability to win.

Prepaid Group Legal Aid Plans

Wealthy people can, of course, afford to hire attorneys to protect their legal rights, and poor people are often able to obtain help that is free or extremely reasonable from legal aid clinics. But the people in the middle often feel frustrated—the people who cannot afford to hire an attorney for a prolonged court battle, but who do not qualify for free legal aid because of their incomes. Caught in such a situation, many people have hired an attorney on a contingency basis. Others have found it wise to belong to a prepaid legal aid group.

Currently, there are a constantly growing number of legal aid service groups that offer prepaid legal assistance to their members. The system works much like accident or health insurance. The benefits a member receives vary; some groups will handle only a few types of cases or services and some give members no choice as to attorney. Others offer wider services and sometimes gives members the opportunity to choose from among the group's attorneys.

This kind of service can be very useful. Some members arrange for a yearly conference, which can be helpful in anticipating and preventing legal problems before they arise. People who are occasionally involved in legal situations because they own property, wish to alter their wills, and so on might be well advised to investigate such programs.

Free Legal Services

Court costs can be expensive. Legal aid clinics usually charge a very modest fee, generally calculated to correspond to your ability to pay. Sometimes the legal services these clinics perform are completely free.

In almost every part of the United States, legal aid clinics operated *pro bono publico*—for the public good—are available. Your local bar association can help you explore the resources in your area.

AGENCIES AND ORGANIZATIONS

The listings that follow are only some of the major national organizations that may help a woman with a legal problem. For example, the National Organization for Women (NOW) is helpful in virtually every area of women's rights. A number of national organizations have a chapter or branch in most major cities throughout the country, and additional expansion can be expected in most instances.

General Sources

American Bar Association
Law Student Division
2109 Spruce Street
Philadelphia, PA 19103

American Civil Liberties Union
Women's Rights Project
22 East 40th Street
New York, NY 10016

Community Action for Legal Services
335 Broadway
New York, NY 10013

Directory of Women Attorneys in the U.S. (price $10)
Ford Associates, Inc.
701 South Federal Avenue
Butler, IN 46721

N.O.W. Legal Defense and Education Fund
641 Lexington Avenue
New York, NY 10022

Women's Equity Action League
538 National Press Building
Washington, D.C. 20004

Discrimination in Hiring and Promotions

Equal Employment Opportunity Commission
Federal Woman's Program
1880 G Street, N.W.
Room 1232
Washington, D.C. 20506

National Labor Relations Board
1717 Pennsylvania Avenue, N.W.
Washington, D.C. 20570

President's Commission on the Employment of the Handicapped
Women's Committee
Room 7126

U. S. Department of Labor
14th Street and Constitution Avenue, N.W.
Washington, D.C. 20210

U. S. Civil Service Commission
1900 E Street, N.W.
Washington, D.C. 20415

U. S. Department of Labor
Women's Bureau
14th Street and Constitution Avenue, N.W.
Washington, D.C. 20210

Abortion, Birth Control and Related Information

American Civil Liberties Union
Women's Rights Project
22 East 40th Street
New York, NY 10016

National Women's Health Coalition
222 East 35th Street
New York, NY 10016

Planned Parenthood (check for local branch)
810 7th Avenue
New York, NY 10019

Sex Information and Education Council of the U.S.
1855 Broadway
New York, NY 10023

U. S. Coalition for Life Education Fund
Box 315
Export, PA 15632

Women's National Abortion Action Coalition
150 Fifth Avenue
Suite 315
New York, NY 10011

Battered Women

If you are the victim of this abuse, call your local police. Your state, county, or city government may run a shelter for battered women and their children. Check your phone book or call the police department and ask them. The location of these shelters is kept secret so that you cannot be followed there, and frequently shelters arrange to help battered women find training, employment, and legal aid.

Rape

If you have been raped, call the police or nearest law enforcement agency without delay. If necessary, also call an ambulance. But make sure that the attack is immediately reported to the police. Thereafter, you may want to check the white pages of your phone book for a rape crisis center hotline. (The information operator may be able to give you the number.) You may want to have a friend, relative, or member of the rape crisis staff accompany you to the police station, but do not allow this to delay reporting the matter to the police. You can insist on having a woman police officer present if you are examined or questioned. Obtaining police response immediately is often the answer in apprehending and prosecuting the attacker.

Name Change

American Civil Liberties Union
Women's Rights Project
22 East 40th Street
New York, NY 10016

Center for a Woman's Own Name
261 Kimberly
Barrington, IL 60010

Children

A call should be made to the nearest police agency in case of serious child abuse.

Children's Defense Fund
1763 R Street, N.W.
Washington, D.C.

National Center for Child Abuse and Prevention
U. S. Department of Health, Education and Welfare
400 6th Street
Washington, D.C. 20201

Check your local phone book under city, county, and state offices for the numbers of adoption departments, child welfare agencies, and child abuse hotlines.

CONCLUSION

It is unlikely that the law will ever please everyone. We seek the law's intervention when we need help. But we sometimes forget that what is a welcome intrusion for some may be an objectionable intervention for others.

We want to be protected by the law. But at the same time, we do not want to be overprotected. Nevertheless, women will, and should, continue to insist on their legal rights.

The attitudes and needs of society undergo almost constant change. Our legal system must be attuned to these changes to keep up with our needs. But our social and governmental structures are such that changes in the law usually lag behind. Our courts and legislatures usually bring about change only after the need has been clearly demonstrated. Still, our basic system is flexible enough to adapt to our demands.

It is because of our heritage of constitutional liberties that we possess the right to bring about change. Women, no less than men, must expand and preserve their legal rights. Never doubt that rights are both your freedom and your defense. Protect them well and insist that they be used!

Glossary of Legal Terms

Listed here are some of the commonly used legal terms that pertain to women's law. Some of these terms have additional meanings in other fields of law.

Abandonment. The unjustified leaving of one spouse by the other, without the intent to return and without the consent of the other (may also apply to a child); the relinquishment or surrender of property rights; giving up a thing completely.

Abduction. A crime in most states that prohibits: enticing or taking away a woman in order to introduce her to a house of prostitution; taking, detaining, or alluring a minor female, without the consent of her parent or guardian; taking or detaining a woman against her will in order to engage in sexual relations or to be married. Legal requirements for this crime vary from state to state. In most jurisdictions, a violation of abduction statutes is also a violation of kidnapping laws.

Abstract of title. A condensed summary or history of title to a particular piece of real estate. The abstract usually begins with a legal description of the land involved and then shows the original government grant. This is followed by a recitation of all subsequent deeds, mortgages, releases, wills, judgments, mechanic's liens, foreclosure proceedings, tax sales, or any other document that had been recorded about this property. By examining the abstract, it can be quickly determined what incumbrances are outstanding against the property, in the event title is not clear. Abstracts of title are regularly kept current in those states where this system is used. Without the abstract, it might be necessary to search through voluminous county records to sift out the information incorporated in the abstract.

Abuse. Any action that is contrary to right or proper usage or accepted order; to use a thing improperly or excessively, or to use it in a manner contrary to natural or legal rules for its use; the crime of sexually molesting a child.

Abuse of process. The perversion or improper use of a legal process in a way in which it was never intended to be used, for example, a male police officer arresting a woman on a warrant and keeping the woman in the police car for several hours without taking her to jail.

Abutting owner. One whose land touches or joins that of another; sometimes used to describe an owner whose land touches a highway or other public place.

Acceleration clause. A statement or clause in a contract evidencing debt (such as an installment contract or a mortgage), providing that if payment or interest is not paid when due, the entire debt becomes payable immediately. Unless an acceleration clause is incorporated into the wording of the instrument, it would be necessary for the lender to sue for the amount of each payment as it falls due.

Add-ons. New purchases made by an installment buyer before the previously purchased merchandise is completely paid for. This usually requires the drafting of a new installment purchase contract.

Admissible evidence. That evidence properly obtained or collected, and that the judge will therefore allow the jury to consider, if it is pertinent to the issues of the trial.

Agency by necessity. An agency relationship recognized by the courts, which enables a wife to obtain whatever is reasonably necessary for her maintenance and support on her husband's credit. In following this reasoning, the courts state that the situation is an implied agency.

Agent. One authorized to carry on business for another or for a firm.

The general rule of law is that the agent must have authority from the principal before the principal is legally bound or obligated by the agent's acts or contracts. However, this right may be lost by the principal who intentionally, or by carelessness, leads a third party to believe the agent has authority.

Annual percentage rate. The annual cost of credit, expressed as a percentage of the average outstanding credit balance.

Appeal. The procedure by which the decision of a lower court is brought to a higher court for review. The system for taking a case to a higher court is set by the rules of the highest state court, or by rules of the United States Supreme Court in Federal appeals.

Appellant. A party to a legal action who makes an appeal to a higher court.

Appellate court. Any court that has authority to hear appeals from a lower court.

Appellate jurisdiction. The authority and power of a review court (higher court) to take over the adjudication and review of a matter that has been tried in a court of original jurisdiction (trial court, lower court, inferior court, or whatever it may be called). Appellate jurisdiction includes the power to correct errors in judgment of the matter under review and may require the case to be sent back to the lower court for additional clarification of the issues.

Attorney in fact. An individual authorized by law to act for another, either for some specific purpose or to transact business of a general nature. Authority to act in this manner is conferred by a written instrument (see power of attorney). An attorney in fact is actually a kind of agent who handles either a specific transaction or general business for the principal. Any mentally competent adult may serve as an attorney in fact, and the term does not refer to an attorney or lawyer in the usually understood meaning of the word. An individual going around the world on a voyage by ship could leave a power of attorney letter with a trusted acquaintance, instructing him or her to sell a piece of real estate. Acting under this written power of attorney, the acquaintance could sell the property and sign the necessary papers to make the transfer legal.

Appellee. One against whom an appeal is taken. This appeal is against the party to the lawsuit that won the decision in the lower court.

Attorney or *attorney at law.* An individual educated in the legal profession; licensed to practice law; employed to furnish legal advice or to prepare and try a cause (case) in the courts. Also known as a *lawyer, counsel, advocate, legal pleader, legal advocate,* or *legal advisor*; in the United States, all of these terms are used interchangeably to mean an attorney or lawyer. In England and some other English-speaking countries, an attorney may draw up legal papers, prepare the testimony, and conduct legal matters out of court, and an advocate or barrister may conduct the actual trial of the case in court. But in the United States, there are no different types or classes of lawyers.

Attorney of record. The lawyer or attorney whose name is entered on court records as the lawyer representing a client, although a number of other lawyers may be working on the case for the same client. The attorney of record is the attorney the client has designated as the client's agent authorized to accept service of legal papers. The attorney of record is distinguished from an *attorney of counsel,* who is any other lawyer hired by the attorney of record to assist in the case.

Bait and switch. A type of deceptive advertising in which a store will bait a customer into entering the store to get an advertised bargain. Sales personnel will then try to switch the customer to a more expensive item on the claim that the advertised item is unsuitable or sold out. In some jurisdictions, this is a criminal violation if the original item was never really available for purchase at the advertised price, or was different from the advertised item.

Bargain and sale deed. A deed with the seller conveys or transfers real property (real estate) to another. The seller guarantees that he or she has done nothing to cause a defect in the title, while at the same time stating that the seller cannot be responsible should it later turn out that there was some hidden defect caused by a former owner. A bargain and sale deed is roughly the equivalent of a grant deed, which is used in some states. A bargain and sale deed is not a complete guarantee of title such as provided by a warranty deed, but is more protection than a quitclaim deed.

Beneficial interest. The financial advantage, profit, or benefit that results from a contract, an estate, or property, as distinguished from absolute legal ownership itself.

Beneficiary. A person or organization that benefits under a will, trust, insurance policy, or agreement.

Bilateral contract. A contract in which both the contracting parties are obligated under the terms of the agreement to fulfill obligations toward each other, reciprocally. It is a contract that is executory (yet to be completed) on both sides; an agreement where mutual promises are made and accepted. For example, one farmer may promise to harvest the wheat crop of a second party, who promises to deliver three dressed sides of beef to the first.

Cause of action. The subject matter of a lawsuit, a redressable wrong, the right to recover something from another through court action. Although a legitimate cause of action may exist, there may not always be a practical legal remedy.

Caveat emptor. Latin for "let the buyer beware." The ancient rule of commercial law, traceable back at least beyond Roman times, that every purchaser must examine, judge, and look for defects, and that the seller will not be held responsible for them.

Cease and desist. An injunction (order) from a court or an order from an administrative agency of the government to immediately refrain from a specific activity that has been declared illegal or objectionable. For example, a manufacturer producing dangerous or defective toys may be ordered by a court to cease and desist from the manufacturing or distributing of such items.

Chattel. Any kind of tangible personal property except real estate. Any type of property except: intangible personal property, such as stocks and bonds (the paper is not value, it simply represents value); or the freehold or ownership in land. For example, cattle and horses are chattels. In fact, the term *chattel* derives from an old French word for cattle, an early symbol of wealth.

Chattel mortgage. A loan arrangement for borrowing with chattels pledged as security. The laws of the various states vary regarding the lender's rights in foreclosing.

Civil case. A lawsuit or legal action undertaken in civil (not criminal) court. It is usually filed to compel payment or money damages, seeking the correction, recovery, or establishment of private wrongs in a civil dispute (not a crime or misdemeanor). In some instances, a court injunction may be requested along with money damages. An injunction is usually a court order directing the correction of wrongful acts or restricting the continuance of such action. A civil case is usually presented for trial by written allegations or claims made by the plaintiff in a petition called a *complaint.* Denials or answers are then filed in written form by the defendant through an attorney.

Chose in action. The right to sue for damages; a right of action not yet reduced to possession or judgment, but recoverable in a lawsuit; a right to collect a debt, demand, or damages; sometimes includes not only the right of action, but also the thing that forms the subject matter of that right, such as a written contract, stocks, or bonds.

Clear title. Title to property that is free of incumbrances, obstructions, or limitations of any kind. For example, a tract of land that has no outstanding mortgage, lien, or claim of any kind against it.

Closed-end credit. Credit contracts that specify the time period over which the loan or sales credit will be repaid, the total amount due, and the number of payments and due dates on which they fall. Typically, it covers most installment credit and single-payment loans.

Cloud on title. Any outstanding incumbrance, claim, or charge against a parcel of real estate. An unpaid tax lien, unsatisfied mortgage, or a previous deed granted for all or part of the property would constitute a cloud on title.

Cohabit. To live together as husband and wife in a sexual sense.

Collateral. Property that the borrower pledges to the creditor to secure debt payment. If the loan is not repaid, the lender (creditor) can look to the collateral to recover all or part of the debt.

Contract. A binding agreement that spells out the terms and conditions of an agreement or business transaction. It is an agreement by which each party is bound to do or to refrain from doing some act, and each acquires a right to what the other promises or performs. A one-sided agreement is not a contract, as it lacks *consideration*.

Conveyance. A legal instrument or document by which title to real estate is transferred; the transfer of the title to real estate from one person or classes of persons to another.

Cosigner. An individual who signs as responsible for a loan or other credit obligation, thereby being required to pay in case of default by the primary debtor.

Counsel or counselor (counsellor). See attorney.

Credit scoring. An internal screening or evaluation of credit applications used by some creditors to determine credit worthiness. The system gives points for the credit applicant's specific characteristics, such as income and number of dependents.

Deed. A legal document by which ownership of land is transferred from one owner or seller (the grantor of a deed) to a new owner. A deed is a conveyance of realty, that is real estate or land, and not personal property or intangibles. Normally, a *bill of sale* or a sales contract transfers ownership of personal items. The essential difference between a deed and a will is that the former transfers a present interest in property, while a will passes no interest until the death of the maker.

Disclaimer. A denial, renunciation, or rejection of liability or legal responsibility in advance, in a situation where responsibility would otherwise be due to a wronged party.

Duress. The use of force to compel someone to do something. A physical restraint may also constitute duress.

Earnest money. The payment of part of the purchase price for real estate to bind the sale. This payment is also sometimes called a *binder.* The understanding is usually that the earnest money will be retained by the seller if the buyer backs out before the sale is completed. If the buyer produces the remainder of the purchase price and meets other terms of the sale, the earnest money is applied as part payment of the purchase price.

Easement. An interest in land owned by another, which interest permits the holder to make a specific use of the land. For example, a man may own two lots, one of which does not have access to a public road. He may sell the lot that has no access, granting an easement across his other lot to the buyer. This would allow the buyer to use a reasonable part of the second lot as a roadway in order to reach the street. If the owner should eventually sell the second lot, the easement across it would continue. Some easements are granted to public service companies, such as an easement for the erection and maintenance of power poles for the installation of an electric line. An easement may be created by an express grant in a deed or contract. If trespassers are allowed to pass over property as a regular practice, the owner may eventually not be able to prohibit the general public from making use of the land in this manner. Laws in this regard vary from state to state.

Embezzlement. The fraudulent appropriation of property or money entrusted to one's own use or benefit. In other terms, the unlawful appropriation or taking of personal property of another by an individual who has gained rightful possession because of employment or by a trust relationship with the owner. The distinction between larceny (theft or stealing) from embezzlement is that in embezzlement the money is in the rightful possession, but not ownership, of the guilty individual. In larceny or theft, the wrongdoer takes that which is in the possession or control of somebody else.

Escrow. A conditional delivery of something to a third party, to be held until the happening of some event or the performance of some designated act. Perhaps the most common escrow situation involves the delivery of a deed to property to a holder until the person buying the property (the grantee of the deed) makes a specified number of payments on the purchase price. When the payments are made, the holder delivers the deed to the grantee (buyer).

Exemplary damages. Damages awarded to the plaintiff beyond those needed to reimburse for the actual loss. Exemplary damages are granted as punishment, or to make an example of the defendant. *Compensatory damages* cover the actual loss.

Failure of consideration. A term used in contract law to describe a situation in which one party to the contract did not perform in the way promised, or when the goods delivered were not as supposed to be. When there is a failure of consideration, the contract cannot be enforced by the party at fault.

Fraud. Deceit, trickery, or deliberate perversion of the truth in order to induce someone to part with something of value or to give up a legal right. Misrepresentation, concealment, or deliberate non-disclosure of a material fact to induce another to enter a contract or a business deal that will work to a disadvantage.

Garnishee. An individual who holds money or property owing to another, which money is subject to garnishment; the act of serving with a garnishment to attach a debtor's wages.

Garnishment. A statutory proceeding whereby a debtor's wages, property, money, or credits are taken and applied as payment toward satisfaction of a debt.

General assignment for creditors or *general assignment for benefit of creditors.* A transfer of all a debtor's money, property, rights, or other assets to a trustee to liquidate the debtor's affairs and pay off the creditors.

Injunction. An order or writ issued by a judge requiring the individual to whom directed to take some specific action or to refrain from doing a particular thing. In a typical case, an injunction would order an individual to cease a wrongful kind of conduct that is harmful to another. The wrongdoer would be restrained from the continuance of this conduct. However, if there is a continuance, the judge will order the arrest of the wrongdoer for *contempt*. Generally, an injunction will be issued in cases where substantial justice could not be done by waiting for the wrongdoer to go ahead and commit a threatened wrong that may not be adequately compensated for in a claim for damages alone.

Lawyer. See attorney.

Lease. A written agreement for the use and possession of property. A lease is granted for a specified time, for a specified payment. The landlord (lessor or leasor), in effect, rents to the tenant (lessee or leasee) for a set period, with payments usually due on a monthly basis.

Legal age. The age when one is considered an adult, old enough to transact business and handle legal matters, such as make contracts or transfer property. The age of legal responsibility. The legal age varies from 18 to 21, depending on state law. For some specific purposes, such as the right to obtain a driver's license, the age may be set below the legal requirement for adulthood.

Legal aid. A bureau or agency that furnishes free legal assistance to those unable to pay, or who can afford very little.

Legal rights. Claims that are enforceable in court or by legal procedures against individuals or against the community; rights recognized and enforced by law.

Lien. The right to take and hold or sell the property of a debtor as security for the debt. A lien is a right established by law, rather than by an agreement or contract between the parties involved. Examples are a landlord's lien to hold property of a tenant for unpaid rent. Another example is a so-called mechanic's lien, giving an auto mechanic the right to hold an automobile until repairs are paid for. A plumber might also have a mechanic's lien for construction work as a subcontractor. The holder of a lien is usually required to give notice of the claim by recording it in the office of the public recorder or other designated public place. In most states, a mortgage takes precedence over a mechanic's lien.

Majority. See legal age, which has the same meaning in practically all legal situations. Majority means the opposite of *minority*.

Marketable title. A title to real estate that is clear of incumbrances, such being a title that would be accepted as valid by a reasonable, prudent buyer.

Mechanic's lien. A legal claim, usually created by statute, securing priority of payment of the value of work performed and the value of materials furnished in constructing or repairing a building or other structure, or in repairing a vehicle. The right of priority of payment attaches to land, as well as to buildings and improvements thereon. A vehicle mechanic has the right to hold the vehicle until repairs are paid for.

Mortgage. A security arrangement that allows land to be used as security for debt; a transfer or pledge of real property passing conditionally as security; the deed or deed of trust by which this pledge is made; the claim of the lender (mortgagee) on the property.

Mortgagee. One who loans money, obtaining a mortgage as security.

Mortgagor. One who pledges property in a mortgage as security for a loan on this property.

No fault insurance. An insurance system that seeks to have automobile accident victims compensated for their losses without regard to their degree of negligence or fault in an accident. The no fault system also seeks to minimize the number of lawsuits by limiting recovery to actual economic losses such as medical expenses, wages and salary, and other real costs, eliminating payments for pain and suffering. States with no fault systems have varying laws.

Nominal damages. A trifling sum of money (often $1) awarded to the plaintiff in a lawsuit where there was no substantial loss or injury, but where the law recognizes a wrong was done, however technical.

Open-end mortgage. A mortgage that provides security for additional advances of money that may be loaned to the debtor (mortgagor) after the mortgage has already gone into operation.

Ordinary creditor. A creditor who has no special preference in the order in which debts are paid by a debtor. Ordinary creditors are generally entitled to be paid only after payment to secured creditors, such as holders of a mortgage or a lien.

Power of attorney. A formal document by which one person gives legal power to another to perform a specific act or to transact general business for the former. It is, in effect, a contract of agency. The person designated to act for the principal may be any legally and mentally competent adult and may not necessarily be a lawyer or attorney at law. The person who holds this power is sometimes called *private attorney* (see also attorney in fact).

Prepayment penalty. A charge sometimes made for paying off a loan prior to the due date. The charge is usually a percentage of the balance, such as 1 percent. A prepayment penalty is sometimes called an *acquisition charge.*

Purchase money mortgage. A mortgage given concurrently with a sale of land by the buyer to the seller on the same land to secure all or part of the purchase price.

Quiet title. A lawsuit or legal hearing to establish title to real property. It is an action that brings into court an adverse claimant and compels him or her to establish such claim to the land or thereafter stop asserting it.

Quitclaim deed. A deed that transfers to the buyer only such rights or property title as the seller (grantor) had at the time the deed was delivered. In most instances, a quitclaim deed may transfer ownership or title just as effectively as any other type of deed. But if there should be a defect (see cloud on title), a new purchaser buys subject to the existing defects in title. In buying under a quitclaim deed, the burden is on the purchaser to find out whether there are claims or incumbrances against the real estate in question.

Realty. Used synonymously with real property.

Recklessness. Conduct amounting to more than carelessness or negligence; wanton disregard for the probability of injurious consequences to others; heedlessness.

Reconveyance. The transfer of title of real estate from the owner to the preceding owner. This particular type of transfer is commonly used in those states where a debt is satisfied under a *deed of trust.* In a typical situation of this kind, a trustee holds title to land put up as security by an individual who borrowed under a deed of trust. When the loan is paid off, the trustee gives a reconveyance back to the original owner.

Recording. The process of filing certain real estate agreements and other legal documents with an official recorder. The purpose of this filing is to legally establish the existence of those agreements or documents and to place all others on notice of their existence, along with the legal implications of their existence. For example, the recording of a mortgage on a farm places any other lender on notice that the first mortgage would have a prior claim on the security of the land.

Retaliatory eviction. An eviction by a landlord prompted by, or as a reprisal for, complaints of a tenant about unsanitary or unsafe conditions on the premises. An eviction of this kind is usually grounds for a damage suit against the landlord, although state laws differ.

Revolving credit. A credit arrangement that allows the borrower to charge or borrow up to a credit limit, with no specific repayment period. Finance charges are assessed on the unpaid balance each month, and a minimum monthly payment is required.

Search of title. An examination of official records and registers made in connection with a contract for the purchase of real estate. This is done to ascertain the existence of mortgages, liens, unpaid taxes, or any other cloud on the title to the property.

Security interest. Any interest in property, real or personal, that secures payment of a debt or performance of an obligation. A mortgage and a mechanic's lien would be examples of a security interest.

Strict foreclosure. A procedure for the foreclosure of a mortgage that vests title to the property in the holder (mortgagee) on default of payment. This foreclosure takes place automatically, without any sale of the property or without the debtor being allowed to exercise the *right to redemption*, as is provided in most mortgages.

Sublease. An underlease; a lease by a tenant of all or part of an already leased premises to another individual. The sublease may be for a shorter term than that held by the occupant under the primary lease (lessee). Some primary leases specify that the property may not be sublet under any conditions. It is best to discuss this problem with the landlord prior to giving a sublease, unless such activity is provided for in the primary lease.

Tax deed. A deed given by the government to a new owner following the forced sale of property for nonpayment of taxes.

Tax lien. A claim against real property (real estate) that arises in favor of the taxing agency (municipality, county, state, or federal government) from tax assessments against the property. If the lien is not paid when due, the taxing agency may sell the property to satisfy the lien.

Tenancy by the entirety. A type of joint ownership by a husband and wife that is used in a number of states. Title is acquired by the marriage partners jointly. Upon the death of either spouse, his or her interest automatically passes to the survivor. Ownership of this kind cannot be terminated without the consent of both parties, and the property cannot be mortgaged or transferred without the written approval of both. This kind of ownership is sometimes called *tenancy by the entireties*.

Tenancy for years. A rental arrangement for a fixed period of time, even though the time may run for less than one year.

Tenant at sufferance. A renter of property who began possession in a legal manner, but who has continued to occupy after the termination of a rent or lease agreement. Technically, a tenant at sufferance is not a tenant of anyone. The landlord may elect to treat such an occupier as a trespasser and demand possession of the property. A demand of this kind will be enforced by the courts. The only duty owed to this occupier by the landlord is not to wantonly or willfully injure the occupier or the occupier's personal property. In some states, the landlord may eject and sue to obtain double or treble rent. If the landlord elects to treat the occupier as a tenant, as by accepting rent at the rate previously paid, the *tenancy at sufferance* comes to an end, and the occupant becomes a tenant at will or a *periodic tenant.*

Tenant at will. One who holds possession of property by permission of the owner, but without any fixed term of years. The arrangement may be terminated at will by either party. Statutes in most states require the landlord to give 30 day's notice in order to terminate. This is the common month-to-month rent arrangement throughout the United States, but is being replaced by year-to-year leases in many areas.

Tenement. Any kind of property that is held by a tenant. The legal meaning is, therefore, somewhat different from the commonly accepted usage of this term. In a legal sense, a tenement may be an elegant mansion, a slum apartment house, or a franchise that is rented to a tenant.

Tenure. The act of holding or occupying, especially land or real estate.

Title. The joining of all the elements constituting legal ownership. It is the means whereby the owner of lands has just possession of the property. Title is sometimes defined as the outward evidence of ownership, as well as the right of full possession, use, and enjoyment of property.

Tort. An injury of a private or civil nature, other than one arising from a breach of contract. A tort is the actionable wrong usually associated with consumer loss or harm resulting from a defective or dangerous product—in short, it involves product liability. In describing a tort, the courts usually say that there must be a wrongful act or commission, coupled with a resulting injury to some person. The injured victim has the right to sue for the damage that results. Corporations are responsible for the torts of their employees committed within the scope of their employment. The more common torts arise out of negligent use of an automobile, assault and battery, or injuries arising from negligent maintenance of store premises available to the public, or from selling adulterated products that cause injury and the like.

Trust deed. A document by which one individual transfers the legal ownership of real estate and what is on the land to an independent trustee to be held until a debt on the real estate is paid off. In short, a deed of trust performs the same security function as a mortgage; however, some different legal implications are involved in foreclosure.

Vested interest. A presently existing fixed right of future enjoyment or use of property. It is an established property right, not dependent on anything. For example, an individual may sell you a lot with a garage on it, delivering you a valid deed. You have a vested interest in the lot and garage at that time. This is true, even though one of the conditions of sale is that the seller is entitled to garage an antique car there for the next year.

Vested right. A legal right that is absolute and not subject to any conditions. It is the certainty of enjoyment that distinguishes a vested right from a contingent interest in property.

Void contract. A contract that is regarded as never having had any legal effect. This results from a situation in which the parties went through the form of making a contract, but in the eyes of the law none was ever made. This is because some essential element of the contract was left out. An agreement of this kind is considered as void from the outset, creating no legal rights at any time. Either party may ignore such an agreement.

Voluntary lien. A lien placed on property with the consent of the owner, or as a result of a voluntary act of the owner. Some liens of this kind arise automatically by operation of law; others come out of an agreement between the parties

Warranty. A statement, representation, or claim made by a seller to a buyer as part of a sale. It includes the seller's claim that the product is fit for use and is a representation concerning the kind, type, quality, and ownership of the thing being offered for sale. There are other warranties that arise by implication, even though the seller may make no claims whatever. These are so-called implied warranties, through which the buyer is entitled to believe the product will fit the performance or specifications that are normally expected of an article of the kind being sold.

Warranty deed. A legal document by which ownership of real estate is transferred from one owner to another. In giving a warranty deed, the seller does two things: (1) transfers the seller's ownership of the property, and (2) legally agrees to defend the validity of that title forever for the benefit of the purchaser. A warranty deed gives the buyer the right to collect from the seller if anyone ever subsequently establishes a claim or cloud on the title to the property. A warranty deed is sometimes called a *general warranty deed.*

Wrongful death statutes. State laws that allow the dependents of one wrongfully or negligently killed to sue for civil damages. The theory here is that the cause of action died with the victim, but that the victim's dependents have a new cause of action.

Index